Hey, You...
Don't Stand Out – Get Out!

The PersonalSuccess Marketing 40/20/40 System To Rescue The Highly-Trained Professional

By Dr. Marc Kossmann and Charlie Seymour Jr

Break Free From The TimeTrap Plateau, Conquer The Online Jungle, and Head For The Summit Of Your Career

Direct Marketing LLC endorses the information the organization or website may provide or recommendations it may make, unless otherwise stated. It should also be noted that Internet website links referred to in this publication owned and operated by third parties may cease to function, change, or disappear between the date when this work was written and the date when this work was read.

Online Direct Marketing LLC may be compensated by third parties or receive free review copies of materials – you are cautioned to make up your own mind about any product or service recommended herein. Those making testimonial statements probably received advanced or free copies of our materials so they could judge the work or they knew one of the authors before this book was written and are making judgements based on their history with that author.

Table Of Contents

What They Say About Dr. Marc and Charlie vii

Acknowledgements xv

Introduction xvii

The 40/20/40 System xix

Is This Book For You? xxii

Move Forward xxiii

PersonalSuccess Marketing xxiv

So Where Do You Start? What Is The Next Step? xxv

Section I – Maximillion's Tale 1

Chapter 1 – Belief 3

Chapter 2 – The Stranger 9

Chapter 3 – On The Garden Path 17

Chapter 4 – Alchemy 23

Chapter 5 – The Forest 29

Chapter 6 – The Dragon 43

Chapter 7 – The Return 49

Section II – Max's Dilemma 53

Chapter 8 – The Jungle 55

Chapter 9 – Lost 63

Chapter 10 – Max's Dilemma Revealed 69

Chapter 11 – A New Direction 75

Section III – The 40/20/40 System 85

Chapter 12 – Time For A Change 87

Where We've Been 87

What Went Wrong? 88

The Online Jungle 90

Can Pain Be A Good Thing? 92

Where We Are Going 93

The Value Of Time 95

40/20/40 Equals 100 Percent Transformation 96

How Hard Is Change? 99

Chapter 13 – Don't Stand Out – Get Out! 101

Professional (Technician) to Entrepreneur 101

Mindset 103

Don't Stand Out – Get Out! 106

Create Your Own Legend 108

PersonalSuccess Branding 109

Chapter 14 – The Universe Model – The 20 113

The Universe Model Of Social Media Marketing 114

The Sun 116

The Planets 117

The Stars 118

Think In Straight Lines, Not Circles 119

Rules Of The Road 120

Why Social Marketing? 121

How Can I Ever Find The Time To Do All This? 122

Chapter 15 – Making The Shift – The Final 40 125

The Shift – Part I: Entrepreneur to Infopreneur 126

Capture 129

Package 134

Video 135

Audio Podcasts 136

Blog Posts 137

The Magic Of Packaging! 138

The Shift – Part II: Infopreneur to Infopreneur on Steroids! 140

Market 142

Syndicate 145

Automate (With Systems to Free Your Time) 146

Outsource 148

The Wealth of Time 150

Section IV – Where IS My Summit? 153

Chapter 16 – DreamDestination 155

Why? 155

Charlie on how TimeFreedom leads From Success To Significance: 162

Bill Books It Big 162

Mike and Vivian Reach Out – Way Out 163

Dr. Marc and Charlie Follow The Lead Of Bill And Mike 166

Now It's YOUR Turn – Your DreamDestination Is Waiting 168

About the Authors 171

What Is PersonalSuccess Marketing? 175

What They Say About Dr. Marc and Charlie

"The man is brilliant..."

"I just heard Charlie Seymour Jr give an AMAZING talk. The man is brilliant, he's a marketer; if you need help getting your business to the next level, you call him."

Jim Palmer
NoHassleNewsletters.com

"...improve your performance and boost your income."

"This fast-moving, entertaining book shows you how to break loose from the past, improve your performance, and boost your income."

Brian Tracy
Brian Tracy.com
Best-selling author of **Goals**, **How The Best Leaders Lead**, and 25 other best selling books.

"Dr. Marc and Charlie show you how to do that."

"Rainmakers get off the TimeTrap Plateau headed for their personal summits. Dr. Marc and Charlie show you how to do that."

Jeffrey J. Fox
FoxAndCompany.com
Jeffrey J. Fox is the author of best-sellers, **How To Be A Fierce Competitor** and **How To Become A Rainmaker**, and many more!

"This charming, fun and easy to read book is truly a gem!"

"Wow! Thanks to Charlie and Dr. Marc I have had a glimpse of the summit and I am psyched! They have provided me with a map. I am ready to fight my dragon. I am learning the importance of knowing and sharing my own legend. I am confident that with the guidance of the map drawn by Charlie and Dr. Marc and by using the tools found both in this book and on the PersonalSuccess Marketing website, I will find my way out of the Online Jungle, climb past the Plateau, and reach the Summit of my DreamDestination!

"This charming, fun and easy to read book is truly a gem! I have already begun reading it for the 3rd time and each time I find more guidance and insight than I did before. Do not wait a moment longer to order this book and sign up on their website PersonalSuccessMarketing.com. Join me, and hundreds of others, as Charlie and Dr. Marc guide us on the journey of our lifetimes!"

Rie Brosco
Owner/Professional Organizer
RieOrganize! iReOrganize.com

"Dr. Marc is a very good business man"

"Dr. Marc is a very good business man, always looking to help people that really want to better themselves. Very outgoing and trustworthy. I would recommend you talking with Marc if you are looking to change your profession and looking for new horizons."

Mario Tagliaferri
West Chester, PA

"This book is an easy read and is jammed with good ideas to improve businesses for all professionals."

"Charlie is a devoted Glazer-Kennedy Insider's Circle student who puts our teachings into practice. This book shows you how to Get Out from the crowd and use Information Products to build a well-oiled business. He has attended more GKIC-Philly meetings than any other member, and it's clear he's learned a lot. This book is an easy read and is jammed with good ideas to improve businesses for all professionals."

Dan S. Kennedy
NoBSBooks.com
Dan Kennedy is the author of the popular No B.S. book series; co-author with Chip Kessler of **Making Them Believe**; co-author with Sidney Barrows of **Uncensored Sales Strategies.**

"MUST READ! ... Look Out!"

"MUST READ! When a clinical psychologist who is an entrepreneur and an MBA marketer who is an infopreneur join forces – Look Out! Dr. Marc Kossmann and Charlie Seymour Jr have written a fun book loaded with great marketing tips. They studied authors such as Jeffrey Gitomer, Seth Godin, Ken Blanchard, and my personal favorite, someone with whom I worked with for 3 years to help build his brand and multi-million dollar empire, T. Harv Eker."

Stefanie Hartman, TV Personality, Publisher, 'Revenue Marketer to the Stars'
StefanieHartman.com

"Through their story-telling you'll see ways to Get Out of the center of your business"

"Dr. Marc and Charlie loved my **The Millionaire Maker's Guide To Creating A Cash Machine For Life** and use a few of their own great techniques in this book. Through their story-telling you'll see ways to Get Out of the center of your business or practice, conquer the Online Jungle, and head for the summit of your career."

Loral Langemeier, CEO/Founder of Live Out Loud, Best-Selling author of the **Millionaire Maker** 3-book series and **Put More Cash In Your Pocket.**
LiveOutLoud.com

"...get Charlie's and Marc's new book — and don't get ageeta: these guys know what they're doing!"

"When I started the marketing of my book, **Gravy Wars: South Philly Foods, Feuds & Attytudes**, I turned to Charlie Seymour Jr for advice about Social Media Marketing. He was generous with his time and specific in his suggestions. As passionate as I am about food, family, and friendships, Charlie is passionate about marketing, Internet list building, and using Facebook to improve your sales: his advice was right on target.

"His new book presents his "Universe Model of Social Media Marketing" as the "20" in his 40/20/40 System that he and Dr. Marc Kossmann have created. If you want to USE the Internet and not feel trapped in the Online Jungle, get Charlie's and Marc's new book — and don't get ageeta: these guys know what they're doing!"

Lorraine Ranalli
GravyWars.com

"Charlie's inspiring business concepts, marketing skills, and unflappable energy proved that anyone, given the right resources, support and optimism, can achieve beyond one's wildest dreams. I will always be grateful to Charlie for these gifts"

"When I first was approached by Charlie Seymour Jr to collaborate on a project almost four years ago, I jumped at the chance. I was a new copywriter then, and anxious to prove myself and build my client base. Little did I know what a fantastic collaboration it would become!

"Charlie was not only warm, generous and intelligent, but he taught me so many things, unknowingly giving me the confidence I needed to produce 150% every time. Throughout the many projects we worked on together, I found myself gaining greater insights into Internet marketing, and learned that stepping slightly outside my comfort zone was not scary, but empowering.

"Charlie's inspiring business concepts, marketing skills, and unflappable energy proved that anyone, given the right resources, support and optimism, can achieve beyond one's wildest dreams. I will always be grateful to Charlie for these gifts, and look forward to partnering with him for many years to come."

Victoria Ipri
Owner, The Confident Copywriter
TheConfidentCopywriter.com

"Marc and Charlie are possibility thinkers, guiding members to realize the potential within their businesses."

"Marc and Charlie are possibility thinkers, guiding members to realize the potential within their businesses. The members – open, receptive and sharing – all want more. They realize that to get more they have to give more. I'd encourage anyone seeking to integrate social media marketing into their business model to experience what Marc and Charlie are creating."

Charles Timmins
SixFigureCareerMastery.com

"When Charlie speaks, people tend to shut the hell up and LISTEN! And why might this be? Because unlike a good many "experts," Charlie knows what the heck he's talking about."

"I've been a member of GKIC-Philly for about 18 months and from the beginning, Charlie Seymour Jr. stood out. Friendly, knowledgeable, out-going, and larger-than-life, Charlie's always entertaining and the epitome of the marketing professional. Charlie's been there for me when others could not or would not help. He's been a personal supporter, and an advocate, and an advisor.

"When Charlie speaks, people tend to shut the hell up and LISTEN! And why might this be? Because unlike a good many "experts", Charlie knows what the heck he's talking about.

"Recently, his advice turned my first foray into online video from an overly long, needlessly plodding snooze-fest into a shorter, tighter, and a far more visually compelling production. "In business and marketing, it's not easy to read the label when you're inside the bottle and there are times when I've been convinced that Charlie's blessed with x-ray vision.

"If you're not sure about a marketing issue, if you need a second opinion, or, indeed, a FIRST opinion, stop! Take stock, and listen to Charlie Seymour Jr. Trust me, you'll thank me for this one day."

Gary Bloomer
The Direct Response Marketing Guy™
GaryBloomer.com

"...you would have been awestruck by the implementation, results, progress, and know-how of keynote speaker and chapter member Charlie Seymour, Jr."

"If you could have been a fly on the wall at last month's primary chapter meeting, you would have been awestruck by the implementation, results, progress, and know-how of keynote speaker and chapter member Charlie Seymour, Jr. Charlie showed and described his 10-step, Kennedy-style, direct marketing sequence that has taken his photography business to new heights. If you're reading this newsletter and still on the fence about becoming a chapter member, Charlie is just one example of the level of experience and 'massive action' we have in our growing group."

From the Desk Of Mike Capuzzi

"I have known Charlie for a few years now and would highly recommend more business owners, entrepreneurs and professionals to PAY ATTENTION to what he has to say......the man is brilliant."

"Great commentary guys, I love the back and forth video series. Keep on delivering the Personal Success nuggets of wisdom. I have known Charlie for a few years now and would highly recommend more business owners, entrepreneurs and professionals to PAY ATTENTION to what he has to say......the man is brilliant.

"As long as I have known him he has always over-delivered when it comes to content, value and insight. I look forward to getting to know more about you, Dr. Marc, and am on my way to Amazon to get my own suction cam. Just the fact that you have teamed up with Charlie tells me that you are a smart entrepreneur and will probably be contributing some great nuggets of wisdom as well."

Justin Stranere
Your Trusted Authority in Real Estate Finance
BucksCountyLoans.com

Acknowledgements

Dr. Marc Kossmann and Charlie Seymour Jr have been blessed by many people in the creation of this book including Patty Lunt, our editor, writing assistant, and friend; Laura Scartozzi, our barista turned illustrator; all the professionals we have known over the years who have shared their stories, AchePoints, and frustrations about how trapped they feel in their businesses; coaches, mentors, and marketing gurus who have shown us great wisdom; lots of people who have encouraged us through their comments and testimonials; all those who have reviewed copies of The Book and have given us guidance, suggestions, and testimonials; and our families who have understood that free-spirited entrepreneurs like us need energy to grow, love and support to give life true meaning, and room to spread our wings in pursuit of our DreamDestinations.

The characters in this book come from the fertile minds of Dr. Marc Kossmann and Charlie Seymour Jr (with an assist from Patty Lunt) and do not represent anyone alive or dead; *or* maybe they represent *all* of us.

Introduction

Right now, you are trapped at the center of your business. You are a professional and most likely one who provides *a service* to your clients, customers, or patients. You are not new to your field and you are not new to the demands of running your business.

You *are* your business. One of the problems with this is that your business has no value without *your* actual presence. It has no intrinsic value, so you are locked in a model that requires you to sell your time for money which has you chained to your business: if you step away, the income ceases.

In that model, you can only increase your income by working more hours (and you don't have *more* hours) or by increasing the fee you bill for each of those hours (and let's face it: how much higher can they go?) or both. That's why you find yourself on a 60 to 80 hour-a-week treadmill that seems to move faster and faster.

So what happened to the "happily ever after" part that comes at the end of the tale? Why all this frustration? Why are you feeling so trapped and, perhaps, a little lost?

We have some bad news for you: what happened, in part, is that you were handed a flawed map when you started your journey. Instead of leading on to the summit of your career, your map created an illusion. You could see your summit getting closer, only to discover that you had arrived on a plateau. There was no way forward from there.

We call it the TimeTrap Plateau because your map taught you to trade your time for money. And to get ahead in your professional work, your map told you to place yourself at the center of your business, working so hard for so long that the circles you ran around yourself dug a deep moat. And now the momentum of life keeps you trapped at the center of your business.

You followed your map exactly where it led you, but to make matters worse a new problem has developed: stuck on the TimeTrap Plateau you are now surrounded by the Online Jungle.

The world around you changed so fast that it has been nearly impossible for you to keep up. Your focus has necessarily been on maintaining your skill and level of expertise within your profession. The problem is that, in the meantime, there has been a revolution in the technological platform upon which all businesses must now market themselves. What was once The Forest you passed through as a dragon slayer (when you received your professional training) is now The Jungle – The Online Jungle... and the business tools you learned "back then" no longer work now.

The time has come for you to acknowledge that 13-year-olds are better equipped for the world of Web 2.0 and social media marketing than you are. You need help *now*.

The old paradigm was about working hard and sacrificing so that you could reach for the "Golden Years" of retirement. (You could be dead before then!) We say, "Thank you, but no." We say break free now, reclaim control over your time, and re-invest your time into what you really care about.

Look, it's not your fault. After all, in your professional training, exactly how many hours were spent teaching you the **business** of your profession? Most of us focused on the technical skills, the **art** of our profession, with little training or warning about the business model.

Something was lost along the way.

Once upon a time you had a glimpse of a Summit, something higher and greater than this plateau where you have become stuck. This is about starting the second half of your career. This is where you discover that the best is yet to come. But you simply can't do this by working 60 to 80 hours a week in your professional business. We will show you how to break free and hold on to your SummitSight™.

Let's face it, you have paid your dues. You have acquired skill and expertise, and you have achieved relative success. We believe, however, that by mid-career it no longer makes sense for you to sell only your professional and technical expertise one hour at a time. You did enough of that to become the expert that you are now.

PersonalSuccess Marketing is as much (if not more) about the psychology of success as it is about marketing. It's time to expose some of the flaws that are built right into the core of the business model within which you currently work.

We will show you how to make money from your expertise *independent* of your time. You will learn how to create sources of recurring value, earning you more money by working fewer hours.

Yes, really.

The 40/20/40 System

At PersonalSuccess Marketing, our 40/20/40 System™ equips you with maps, tools, and a powerful system so that you can systematically buy back your time to start dreaming a bigger dream – you will have the freedom and vision to define and pursue your true DreamDestinations™, the ultimate achievement of your life's work.

First, just what is the 40/20/40 System? It is the total transformation of your business model and philosophy. The first 40 percent is a focus on a psychological change in your professional identity. The next 20 percent is the building of a powerful online marketing system. The final 40 percent is a shift in the very nature of what you do with your professional and technical expertise. Together, the 40/20/40 System equals a 100 percent transformation.

Get Started. You need to build a bridge over the moat you dug around yourself so you can Get Out of the center and move to the edge of the plateau. Without this preliminary work, there is no point to thinking about heading into the Jungle.

This is the work of the First 40 in our 40/20/40 System. And yes, breaking free from mental traps is fully 40 percent of your journey. First, you must go inside yourself to understand the pain and frustration that is building in you. Then, really acknowledge feeling trapped at the center of your business where everything depends upon your immediate physical presence. If you are self-employed, if you *are* your business, then your business owns *you*: you need to reverse that to become the *owner* of your business.

You must Get Out. You must get out of the center, and you must make a psychological shift to get out from seeing your profession as being a significant part of how you define yourself.

We call this process Create Your Own Legend. It is about finding your unique story which distinguishes you from simply being like everyone else (some call that "being a commodity"). Your professional identity tells the story of your *group,* but if that is *your* story, you will forever struggle – let's face it: it's hard to stand out when you appear to be just like everyone else.

Once you have a good map and a guide, then it's time to arm yourself with the right tools. We are here to outfit you with what you need as you move off the TimeTrap Plateau and through the Online Jungle.

Go Through The Online Jungle. But if you only need to learn how Facebook, Twitter, blogs, or video marketing works: there are plenty of how-to-market-online books for you – this is not the book for you. We take this further. These tools, together with the strategic understanding of how information moves through the 'universe' of social media, represent 20 percent of the journey you take when you want to break free and head for the summit of your career.

The story that you created in the First 40 – where you Create Your Own Legend – becomes an organizing framework for communication with the social community you will build using the Universe Model of Social Media Marketing™. This is the new world of marketing. Mastering the Online Jungle is about becoming a master builder of networks – networks of relationships with customers, clients, referral sources, and patients. And social media tools need to be combined with good old-fashioned relationship-building strategies.

Our focus is on the psychology of relationship building which *is* the psychology of marketing. We combine that with the technology of marketing and the use of online tools as a means of communicating with customers, clients, and referral sources. We make sure that high touch is delivered by high tech.

So, if you are prepared to take this full journey, then we will show you what tools you need (and those you can skip), how they all work together (through our Universe Model of Social Media Marketing), and how you can transform the marketing of your business. This is the 20 percent in our 40/20/40 System.

Make The Shift. The final 40 percent of the 40/20/40 System relates to a change in the definition of what your business really is, what it does, and what it produces. We will show you how to move you off The Plateau, out of The Jungle, and on to The Summit of your career.

The Final 40 becomes the strategic marketing plan that you are going to pump through the 20 percent that is your marketing system.

Once you make that critical change from *being* the professional to being the *owner* of a business that provides professional services, you are ready to move forward. The Shift will now take all of that knowledge, skill, experience, and expertise that you developed in the first half of your career, capture it, and package it into information products. This is The Shift from professional to "Infopreneur."

And by placing knowledge-based products onto the online marketing system you created with the Universe Model of Social Media Marketing, you will become an Infopreneur on Steroids! These are the steroids of automation and syndication that allow your income to break from the stranglehold of your hourly efforts: you no longer trade time for money – you trade knowledge and expertise for money.

Without The Shift of this final 40 percent, you will venture off the plateau, through the jungle, and right back up to a new plateau. This Final 40 leads off the plateau forever. This final Shift is how you reclaim your time: it sets you free from the TimeTrap Plateau. The Shift, the Final 40, is absolutely critical.

Is This Book For You?

The answer is yes if you are a mid-career, mid-life professional, especially one who provides services to clients, customers, or patients, who has discovered that there is a serious problem with the business model that brought you to this point.

You have discovered that you are working long hours (*very* long hours) – hours that you trade for money. You may have discovered that there are no more hours that you are able (or willing) to sell. And you have come up against the ceiling of what the market will bear in terms of the fee that you can reasonably charge for your time. So, you have become stuck on a plateau.

At PersonalSuccess Marketing, we know that once upon a time there was a destination you had in mind. We refer to this as your DreamDestination. And you followed a map that was supposed to lead you to the summit of your career. And that summit was supposed to lead on to your DreamDestination.

But we also have some good news for you: we have a *better* map. One that leads you off this plateau, through the jungle, and up to the summit where you have the clear vision to define and pursue your DreamDestination, the culmination of your life's work.

We are going to free you from the TimeTrap Plateau. To do this you will move out from the very center of your business and you will develop an effective online-marketing platform. On that platform you will begin to deliver your knowledge, experience, and expertise in a form that will free you from simply trading your time for money. You will eliminate the ceiling that is currently capping your income. You will buy back your time and become the owner of a business that generates income independent of your direct, hourly efforts.

Move Forward

We believe that *time* is the true measure of wealth. If you have to keep working 60 to 80 hours a week to keep the cash flowing, then there is a serious problem. When wealth is defined solely in terms of money, you run the risk of losing control of your time. Only with the wealth of time can you be present with your family, travel, and engage in real charitable work.

When you own your time, you can move *from success to significance*. You are free to reinvest your time into areas that have real *meaning* for you. People tend to focus on money and lose sight of the reality that money is a tool whose real value is its ability to leverage time.

When you are at the summit of your career, you systematically buy back your time and really *own* it. You are positioned to take an hour of work and get paid for it many times over. We are here to show you how to buy back your time and accomplish this shift. Time allows you to scan the horizon from the height of the summit, and from this altitude, you have the clear vision to define and pursue your PersonalSuccess DreamDestination.

You will have the control to leverage time to achieve new heights. How will you choose to reinvest this new-found time? What is going to provide your life with real meaning? What is your legacy, and how will you choose to leave your mark in this world? The answers are up to you!

PersonalSuccess Marketing

In the pages that follow, we invite you to have a little fun. You will discover Maximillion's Tale. This is the story of the past. You will then share in Max's Dilemma. This is the story of the present, and we have a feeling that you might just recognize a little of yourself in Max. And finally, we are going to take a deeper look at how we resolve Max's Dilemma and head off to a much brighter future through our 40/20/40 System.

We want you to learn and be entertained through our stories and information. We also want to help you as much as we can.

While this book provides you with the overview of PersonalSuccess Marketing, we invite you to join us at the website where PersonalSuccess Marketing actually lives. The book can't change once printed but the website is where you can become part of a developing community committed to your personal success.

We know that there is some kind of chemical reaction that takes place when you lock an entrepreneurial-focused clinical psychologist and a marketing-crazed MBA in a room for too many hours – and as those hours expand to months and years of meeting and working together, things intensify.

The result is PersonalSuccess Marketing™. This book is a part of that chemical reaction and it's written by two guys who are just like you: professionals who were stuck on a plateau with no way to get off until we discovered the secrets we share here with you.

Discover the whole story at our website, PersonalSuccessMarketing.com, where you will find the living, breathing result of our ongoing work together. It is also where you can join us to become a part of a growing community of professionals and small business owners dedicated to your PersonalSuccess.

At PersonalSuccessMarketing.com you will find a great deal of information to help you (and we've outlined some of it in the appendix of this book: **What Is PersonalSuccess Marketing?**).

So Where Do You Start? What Is The Next Step?

Before you read any further, head right now to our website (PersonalSuccessMarketing.com) to register your contact information in the upper right-hand corner of any page. That will allow us to share with you all upcoming events and important information. That is your next step. Sign Up Right Now!

Then it's time to enjoy Maximillion's Tale, Max's Dilemma, and our 40/20/40 System including how to Get Out and Create Your Own Legend, the Universe Model of Social Media Marketing to take your through the Online Jungle, and then The Shift to take you straight to the top.

So: read on once you are registered at our website. We'll see you at the Summit!

Dr. Marc Kossmann and Charlie Seymour Jr

PS: You'll notice our Shield, so here's a bit of explanation:

The dragon represents the unknown, the venture we all take, what we need to overcome when we head out to get our education, training, experience. It's behind everything we do in our careers.

The bottom quadrant represents all of us – the base, the support, the walled-in city of our minds and the path that leads to it. It's the place where we retreat, but also the place where, when we open to the possibilities of the future, we can succeed as never before.

The left quadrant is the forest – the place we go to slay our own dragon. It represents the past.

The right quadrant is the jungle – the Online Jungle where we each find ourself right now. It represents the present.

The top quadrant is the summit – the Summit of our Careers – where we were headed when our journey began: above the tree line where we can see clearly to get to our DreamDestination.

As our adventure progresses, we fill in the shield, showing you where we are in the story.

All of this will become clearer as you read our book. Read, learn, dream, and succeed!

Section I – Maximillion's Tale

A Long Time Ago There Was A Young Man Named Maximillion…

Chapter 1 – Belief

Maximillion crouched on the earthen floor of his father's smithy, embers drifting through the air like a multitude of fireflies. The steady *clang, clang, clang* of hammer against steel was broken by angry spitting and hissing as hot metal plunged into the tempering basin.

His father darted from station to station, keeping an eye on all the workers, making sure the fire was hot enough and the water was cool enough. Maximillion was tired just watching him. It seemed his father made work as difficult as it could be.

Maximillion considered his tubes of powdered minerals and vials of liquids, absently batting at the occasional ember that ignited his wheat-colored hair. He consulted his battered notebook, tapping his pen against his head as if to knock loose some forgotten tidbit of information.

He'd already tried every conceivable combination of minerals and liquids. But no matter how hard he tried, nothing had served to strengthen the steel used for armor and swords. It was light, but brittle. And brittle steel was useless steel, according to his father.

Maximillion viewed failure as valuable information about what didn't work, what could be eliminated from the equation. But his father saw things differently: it was wasted material, wasted time, wasted effort.

Maximillion was at a loss as to what to try next. His head ached and he was tired. He threw the notebook into the chest used to store his tools.

As it was, the armor was incapable of protecting a soldier from the Warrior King's Army. Strengthen the armor to withstand spears and arrows, and it was too heavy for a man to wear. Another attack from the east was inevitable, and the next time the Prince might not be as lucky as he was the last.

After three years of effort, Maximillion had little to show for his trouble beyond an unwavering belief that he could find a solution to the weight-versus-strength dilemma.

"Still wasting time on your pipe dreams?"

Maximillion looked up to see his father looming over him. He sighed as he rose to his feet, looking the older man in the eyes.

"It's feedback, not failure. What doesn't work brings me one step closer to what will."

His father snorted in response. "Our armor has protected the border for years. Don't know why you think there's need for something besides what we've got."

"Because our defenses were almost breached during the last attack, Father. Because this armor is too heavy for most of the soldiers. Because, last time, our swords were no match for the Warrior King's weapons."

"Bah! This armor's worked for years and will work for years after you and I are gone."

"I don't think so, Father. We may not be so lucky next time the Warrior King attacks. We have to prepare…"

"You're wasting time, as usual. There's an order waiting at the quarry. Get it and get back before dark."

Maximillion sighed. It was no use arguing with his father on this. The man simply didn't see the need to improve on the old technology. The armor and swords had been good enough to defend the kingdom in years past. But his father simply didn't understand, or didn't want to consider the possibility, that they might not be good enough for the future.

Maximillion wanted to shake the old man, to force him to see that times were changing faster than they could keep up. He seemed to have his focus fixated. But instead the young man simply acquiesced. He understood that he needed to show his father rather than try to convince him.

"Yes, sir."

As Maximillion turned to go, his foot caught the corner of a crate half-full of gleaming, freshly forged short swords. He danced to stay upright and succeeded, though he overturned a bucket of ash in the process. He stooped to clean the mess but his father bellowed at him.

"Leave it! Go now and don't dally on the way!"

"Yes, Father."

Maximillion felt the silence at his back. He knew his father and the workers had serious doubts about his suitability to manage the smithy. Truth be told, Maximillion had doubts himself. The Blacksmiths' Guild was highly competitive and his father was constantly in an uproar over who got what contract, the price of materials, getting orders out on time. Life was an endless miasma of dissatisfaction where the smithy was concerned.

Maximillion padded across the loamy road in his knee-high, buckskin boots. The sweet aroma of straw, horse, and leather reached out to him and he quickened his pace. Looking up, he saw the afternoon sky was still bright and clear, with just a hint of a breeze keeping the heat at bay. He unlatched the door that was more gap than wood and entered.

It was dark, but shafts of light filtered through the roof, illuminating countless dust motes floating above. He heard the shuffling of straw and felt the thud of Dora and Nora's heavy hooves as they shifted to see who'd entered their domain. They whickered a soft hello.

Maximillion spoke soothingly to them, stroked their baby-soft noses, felt their hot breath on his hands. He opened the stall doors and both horses followed him to the harnessing area. They stood patiently as the heavy rig was placed on their broad, auburn shoulders, then delicately backed into their places between the wagon's shafts.

Maximillion hopped up on the bare plank that served well enough as a seat and clucked Dora and Nora into motion. The girls, their massive, dappled hips swaying left and right, strained excitedly against the well-oiled harness as they pulled out onto the main thoroughfare.

The street was crowded this afternoon, for it was market week. Vendors from miles around had come with their wares to trade at the MidChester's monthly market and faire. Dora on the left, threw her head up in alarm at the sight of a teetering man balancing five baskets of brightly-dyed cloth upon his shoulders. Maximillion spoke to the horse in a low voice and she dropped her head, but kept a wary eye on the swaying apparition just the same.

There were wagonloads of fruits and vegetables – orange, green, red, and purple – gleaming in the westering sun's lengthening shadows. A family of minstrels followed behind Maximillion's wagon, tinny pipes and off-key voices calling onlookers to the market's festivities. In front of the boarding house, a woman in black and brown sang "A Mother's Lament," wringing her hands as she occasionally broke into sobs.

Maximillion soaked up the sights and sounds of the street. Had the monthly faire always been so exotic, so mysterious? It didn't seem so. Why was today so different?

His eyes darted from singers, to jugglers, to a flock of chickens being herded by two red and white dogs. Their two-legged master sauntered behind, gnawing on a joint of mutton. As Maximillion watched the man and the mutton, his stomach began to grumble, and he realized he hadn't eaten for hours. MidChester Tavern was just ahead. Perhaps it wouldn't hurt to stop for a bite to eat. Maximillion thought of the thick stew and fresh, crusty bread waiting inside, and all else was erased from his mind.

As he tied the team to a gnarled apple tree, he noticed a strange horse at the tavern's hitching post. It was far different from the fat, pampered horses that plied the streets of MidChester. It was a thin animal, but with well-toned muscles that roped beneath its shaggy, chestnut coat. A long scar was scratched down its left haunch, and a bright pink bald patch ran down its left shoulder and neck. The horse kept a cautious eye on the crowd, though none of the hubbub seemed to concern the animal much.

Maximillion's curiosity was piqued. Who rode such a horse?

He must find out.

Chapter 2 – The Stranger

The tavern was dark inside, the odor of beer-soaked dirt heavy in the air. Maximillion stood in the doorway as he waited for his eyes to adjust to the gloom.

At the bar, a wizened, stooped man was spinning a tale of his journey into The Forest.

The Forest. Maximillion's spine tingled at the mere mention of the mysterious land beyond the safety of MidChester's high, strong walls.

The city of MidChester was a remote, bustling, defensive outpost in The Kingdom. Because it shared a border with the Warrior King's lands to the east, it warranted a castle fortress reigned over by one of the King's sons. Couriers rode out three times a day between MidChester and the capitol city to keep the King apprised of the situation on the eastern border. The city itself was an extension of the castle and served as a walled stronghold for a regiment of the King's

Army. To the east, a wide, dark river served as a border between The Kingdom and the lands of a Warrior King.

The Warrior King had tried to invade Maximillion's homeland several times over the years. The invasions hadn't been successful. Yet. It seemed only a matter of time before the superior forces of the Warrior King found a way to breach MidChester's defenses.

On the western side, outside of MidChester's stone walls, lay a vast expanse of green that was the border zone between The Kingdom and The Unknown that extended far up to the north. Soldiers regularly patrolled The Forest edge, but few ventured beyond... as what began as a lush and beautiful forest rapidly transitioned into a dense, dark, and dangerous tangle of trees, underbrush, and brambles.

There were no established roads through The Forest, only hunting trails. Maximillion had only heard rumors of men who had traveled to MidChester from beyond the known territory. And of those traveling out from MidChester into the west, seeking adventure – well... few ever returned.

What if the owner of the strange horse had come from beyond The Forest? What tales he would have to tell!

Maximillion often found himself dreaming of what might lie beyond that forest. Virtually all MidChester families had tales of relatives who had ventured into The Forest and returned with accounts of different languages and cultures, of towering cities, vast lands, and strange rituals. Maximillion was sure that these stories had grown with the telling, as did all legends. But none explained what became of those who had simply vanished into the green.

The tavern door flew open, and silhouetted in the doorway was a tall, lean man. Silence fell over the room as The Stranger strode to the bar and ordered food and drink.

He was tall and muscular, with silver hair that hung past his shoulders. He wore a glistening silver armor breast plate and carried a sword with ornate engravings on the handle. But it was his face that caused the hushed silence. The left side of his face was so badly scarred that all features were obliterated. Where his eye should have been was a soft declivity, covered over with a tracery of fine lines. It looked like a piece of caul fat lay across half his face.

Carrying his bread and ale, The Stranger made his way to a table in the corner. Maximillion did not fight the irresistible urge to follow the man. He was starved for adventure, and this man's face made it clear that he was someone with a tale to tell. But, being a blacksmith's son, he was also quite curious about the armor and sword that were so clearly different from anything he had ever encountered.

Maximillion approached The Stranger, who nodded his assent when asked if the young man could join him.

Maximillion learned that The Stranger was from a distant land to the west, and that as far as he knew, he was the last of his people. The man was evasive about what sort of tragedy had befallen his city. Maximillion respected the man's privacy, so he turned his questioning to the strange metal. The Stranger placed the sword upon the table between them, and Maximillion looked at it with awe. The engraving was complex, but there was clearly a dragon wrapped around some type of tower and what looked like a bolt of lightning striking a crowd of people.

"I've never seen such a blade," whispered Maximillion as he sat on the bench opposite The Stranger. "It's beautiful, yet there's something terrifying about it."

"Its name is Silverthorne."

Maximillion ran his fingers along the blade. He could feel the coiled tension within the blade, like a snake before it strikes.

He noted it seemed to glow from within, like some light source was hidden in the weapon.

"What city do you call home?"

A wistful look played across The Stranger's tortured face. "My home no longer exists."

Maximillion was dying to know more, to know what fate had befallen The Stranger's city and people, but it was clear the man didn't want to speak of it.

"Was this weapon forged in your city?"

"Yes, by my own hand." The Stranger took a mouthful of bread and a swallow of ale. "Pick it up."

The sword had a slight vibration that seemed to come from someplace very deep within. It was warm to the touch, as though someone had been holding it moments before. But Maximillion had seen The Stranger pull the sword out of its scabbard. It should be cooler than the surrounding air, like any self-respecting metal. What amazed Maximillion far more was how little the weapon weighed. The broad sword was lighter than a saber in his hands.

"Amazing," Maximillion murmured, setting the blade on the table. "It's magnificent."

The Stranger pulled out a cloth and polished the sword where Maximillion had touched it. The glow from the blade seemed to soften and deepen.

As someone entered the tavern, Maximillion saw that it was getting dark outside.

Remembering his errand, Maximillion rose to leave, "Will you be in MidChester long?"

"A day or two, no more."

The Stranger pulled a suede pouch from beneath his cloak and tossed it on the table.

"You may find this interesting, young blacksmith," he said, nodding at the pouch.

Maximillion picked up the pouch, tucked it inside his vest, and thanked the man. Any curiosity he had about the bag's contents was immediately forgotten. It was almost dark outside.

His father would be furious.

Maximillion went as quickly as possible to the supply house. The owner was cranky at having to wait so long. Maximillion apologized and loaded the goods in the wagon, then drove Dora and Nora home as quickly as the load and waning light would allow.

When Maximillion returned to the smithy, his father pulled him aside.

"Sit down a moment, son. The men can unload the supplies."

The two men walked over to the bench that stretched along the side of the barn. Maximillion's father eased down onto the seat, rubbing his knees and grimacing.

"I told old man Conroy that you'd be there before dark. Were you?"

"No."

"So what did he say when you showed up late?"

"Nothing much. Just how he was hungry and tired and didn't like to be kept waiting."

"Folks like to do business with people who keep their word. It's called *integrity*. Delivering on your promises means you have integrity. Showing up on time means you have integrity."

"I told him I was sorry. I stopped at the pub to…"

"Son, folks also don't care about you or your life. They care about themselves. All they want to know is how they're affected, or if you can solve their problems for them. If you can't, they'll find someone who can. And before you know it, you're out of business."

Maximillion thought about what his father said. He'd never realized how what seemed like trivial actions could affect the smithy. He'd never thought about integrity before. Now, as he focused on this, he realized how it was the accumulation of small actions, each seemingly trivial, that became the measure of character.

Upon reflection, Maximillion could see why his father was often angry at him. There were two other smithies in town, and both would love to get a shot at the Prince's armor contract. Through his actions, or lack of action, he had been risking his father's business and the livelihoods of all the men who worked there. Maximillion vowed it would never happen again.

The smithy's fires glowed through the night. It took nearly 48 hours of non-stop effort for them to complete the order. Maximillion was resolved to stay and work side by side with his father and the men. His mother came by and made concerned clucking sounds, but Maximillion just smiled and said he wasn't tired.

As he pounded the hot steel with his hammer, Maximillion's fatigued mind wandered off. He thought back to his encounter with The Stranger and dreamed of himself clad in The Stranger's wondrous armor, wandering the deepest regions of The Forest without fear, in search of adventure.

Finally, on the third day after his encounter with The Stranger, Maximillion, his father, and the men loaded the wagon with the freshly-forged weapons and armor. Maximillion's father slapped him on the back and nodded his approval. Maximillion slapped the reins against the horses' dusty rumps. His heart was soaring, not only because he had received his father's approval, but because he might see Katherine today.

Chapter 3 – On The Garden Path

The guards at the castle gate waved him through and made disparaging remarks about his ancestry and his fondness for farm animals. Maximillion just smiled and kept the horses moving. What did he care of the castle guards' opinion of him?

Maximillion stopped Dora and Nora in front of the main barracks, a long, low building painted green, gold, and white, the colors of MidChester. A few soldiers lounged on the long boardwalk that fronted the barracks and gave Maximillion a good taunting as he off-loaded the crates. He paid them no heed. Katherine would be walking the gardens soon, and he missed her terribly.

After emptying the wagon, Maximillion secured the horses and headed toward the gardens that the Prince had generously made available year-round to the public. Maximillion took a turn around the carefully edged path that led to the center of the garden. A forest of topiary animals were frozen in impossible positions in the center of the yard, and in the center of the animals, a three-tier fountain splashed water down from the height of four men.

Maximillion cast his gaze about the garden, hoping to see some sign of movement, but it seemed he was alone.

Maximillion and Katherine had been having these "chance" encounters since they were children. They would often walk together and talk, sharing each other's hopes, fears, and dreams of the future. She was the only person with whom Maximillion shared his dreams of  adventure and his belief that he could create a new kind of metal, lighter and stronger than anything ever created before.

But there was one dream that Maximillion could not share with her. That was his dream that someday she would be his wife, for he loved her beyond measure. It was the silly dream of a blacksmith's son, for she was the Prince's daughter and clearly beyond him.

Katherine's world was the world of ornate gardens, servants, and brocade gowns. Maximillion's was a world of smoke, fire, and metal. The only place their two worlds intersected was here on this garden path.

As Maximillion's thoughts turned dour, Katherine appeared. She carried a bow and quiver, wore leather breaches, knee-high boots, a shirt, and vest. Her long auburn hair was pulled back in a tight bun.

"I surrender," he said, throwing up his arms.

She laughed, a deep, honest sound that made his heart skip a beat.

"Wise choice."

"How goes it in the castle?"

She shrugged her shoulders. "The same today as yesterday. First languages, then history. Then I help prepare the table for the noontime meal, after which I eat the noontime meal, observing all the while proper etiquette and protocol suitable for an affair of state. Then I must recite the names and genealogies of the heads of state for The Kingdom and all its allies...."

Maximillion could hear the weariness in Katherine's voice as she continued.

"I had to clear my head with some target practice." Katherine placed her bow and arrows on a gray stone bench, then adjusted the laces on her boots. "Now I'm going to the river for a nice long swim."

Maximillion raised his brow. "They let you do that?"

Katherine looked up with a set jaw, "I'm not asking for permission." Then she smiled and some of the tension drained out of her. "I'm sorry, Maximillion. I'm not in the mood to be a princess today, but I don't mean to take it out on you."

Maximillion smiled his forgiveness and asked, "Shall we take a turn around the yard?"

She picked up the bow and quiver and threw them over her shoulder. "Today, I'd like to saddle a horse and ride into The Forest and never look back. See what's beyond all that green."

Hoping to take her mind off castle life, Maximillion told Katherine of the order for the Prince, and how they'd worked through two nights to complete it. He told her of the talk with his father, how he now realized that he'd been jeopardizing the shop and its employees for years, and how he was going to change.

As their loop around the garden came back around to the castle gates, Katherine took his hand in hers.

"I'm proud of you. Not many men can see when they're wrong, and even fewer are willing to change their ways."

"Thank you, m'lady."

Maximillion bowed slightly, kissed her hand, and made his way back to the stables. As he drove out of the gates, he turned to see Katherine watching him depart. He waved his hand and she blew him a kiss.

Driving home, Maximillion stopped at the tavern where he'd met The Stranger. He asked the innkeeper if The Stranger was still in town, but no one really knew much of anything about the man or from whence he came. It was only then that Maximillion

remembered the pouch The Stranger had given him. He had simply forgotten about it in the rush to complete the order for the Prince.

He reached into his vest pocket and sat down at the table where he and The Stranger had talked. When he opened the pouch, he found it filled with a fine silver powder that seemed to glow just as The Stranger's armor and sword had. Right away, Maximillion knew that he had work to do.

Chapter 4 – Alchemy

Many weeks passed as Maximillion worked with The Stranger's powder, experimenting with different variations in the ratios he combined. But the result was always the same: light weight, but brittle and lacking strength. Nothing at all like The Stranger's armor and sword had been.

Maximillion pushed back his stool in frustration. Standing up, he jostled the table, sending the pouch skittering onto the floor. In his effort to save the powder, he crashed into the bucket of fresh water set up for tempering his experiments.

The powder, the water, and the earthen floor all came together into a silvery pool of viscous, glowing mud. Maximillion's frustration vanished as he saw what his clumsiness had wrought.

Could the formula be so simple? No iron, no fire – just earth and water? Such basic elements combined with the new substance The Stranger had provided. He'd been trying so hard to use this new element to strengthen the steel, he'd never even considered that he didn't need any metal, just earth and water.

Suddenly, one of his father's sayings popped into his head. "Beware what you search for, because you'll always find it." He'd been suffering his own form of outlook myopia. He had only been searching for an additive to the metal and so he hadn't been open to new possibilities and combinations of materials. What a dolt he'd been! He promised himself he'd always be open to new processes and new ways of thinking, broadening his vision.

The substance was beginning to harden. Maximillion quickly took the mass to the work bench, grabbed his hammer and began pounding out the metal, shaping it into a dagger as it set. There was not enough here to make even a short sword, as he had used up so much of the powder in weeks of experimenting.

Maximillion was amazed at his creation. This dagger had the same ethereal glow as The Stranger's armor and sword. It was amazingly light, as the sword had been. But unlike anything Maximillion had ever been able to forge, this dagger had incredible strength. Nothing seemed able to dull its edge. And even prying up a cobblestone from the street could not flex or break the blade.

After almost four years of experimentation, Maximillion had found success, thanks to The Stranger's gift. But now The Stranger was gone, and there was no more of the wondrous powder available.

Maximillion had never had the chance to ask where it came from, and he had no idea where to find this Stranger. No one had seen him before or since his visit nearly two months ago. After asking around, Maximillion discovered that The Stranger was last seen heading back into The Forest to the west.

How maddening! The answer to Maximillion's prayers for a lighter, stronger metal had been answered, but now he had no more of the magical substance that made the miracle possible. And the man who had given him that substance had vanished into the one place that Maximillion had no chance of finding him.

The solution seemed utterly clear and equally impossible. He had to go into The Forest, find this Stranger, and discover the source of this silver powder.

But how could he abandon his responsibilities at the shop? His father would be alone to deal with the other Guild shops that were just waiting to take advantage of any opportunity to get the Prince's business. Maximillion needed to focus on his responsibilities here at home. That was the answer, then... Maximillion would stay at home to help keep the business strong.

Soon, though, scouting reports began coming in from the east. The Warrior King was preparing to wage a new campaign against The Kingdom, and the word was his forces were stronger and greater in number than anything the King's Army had ever faced before. For the first time, there was real doubt. People were afraid and the fear was a palpable thing. Maximillion could see it on the people's faces, feel it in their clammy hands, and smell it on their breath.

Maximillion was torn. He had promised his father that he would be reliable, responsible, and trustworthy. Yet how could he keep The Stranger's secret to himself? He needed to find more of the magical silver material and make more weapons so the city could be defended. He wanted to talk to his father, but feared he wouldn't get an objective opinion of the situation from the old man.

He knew with whom he needed to speak.

He found Katherine sitting on the bench next to the fountain. She was concentrating on something, and when he neared, he saw it was needlework.

"Hello, Princess."

Maximillion was rewarded with a warm smile. "Maximillion. What a wonderful surprise. I was about to go mad with these blasted pillowcases."

"I need your advice."

Katherine dropped what she was doing and gave Maximillion her undivided attention.

He told her the story of The Stranger, of his gift, and how, after many weeks and a happy accident, he had stumbled across the formula to create superior weaponry. When he finished his tale, he pulled the dagger from his pocket and handed it to the princess.

"Oh, it's so light," Katherine remarked, hefting it with her hand. "Nicely balanced, too."

"Try to pry up a stone," said Maximillion, nodding at the pavers that lined this portion of the garden.

Katherine gave him a sideways look but did as she was bid. She dug in the walkway, leveraging the blade between the stones until one popped out of its mortar. Examining the blade, she whistled. "Impressive. What was that silvery substance that The Stranger gave you?"

"I don't know. I've never seen anything like it before. Have you ever heard of such a thing?"

"No. I've seen some pretty remarkable things at court, but never anything like this." She handed the blade back to Maximillion. "Can you get more?"

"Well, maybe, if I knew where The Stranger had gone."

"You've got to find him."

"But I promised my father I'd be more reliable. I can't just run off and go searching for this man."

Katherine took the young blacksmith's hands.

"Maximillion, I understand your dilemma. But this is bigger than a promise to your father. This is bigger than the smithy. The Warrior King is preparing to cross the river. Our city and all its people are at risk."

Maximillion knew she was right. He had to find The Stranger, even though the successful completion of such an undertaking seemed like an impossibility at the moment.

"You're right, of course."

"We can talk about it on the trail. We've got to get going. Now."

"*We?* You can't go with me."

"Sure I can."

"Katherine, all I know is that I'm heading into The Forest and perhaps beyond. I don't know what waits for me out there, but I don't imagine it's too pleasant. The last thing I need is to worry about keeping you safe."

"You worry about finding The Stranger. I'll worry about staying safe. Whatever you might think about me and my family, know this: we are in service to the people. My life is secondary to their welfare and I will do anything to assure their safety."

Katherine stood up, hands on hips. "So if you think you're going without me, think again. Now let's go find The Stranger and get some weapons made."

Maximillion sighed and stood. He knew he'd never talk Katherine out of going on this journey. Any other time he'd be overjoyed at her company, but now? He had no idea how he'd manage to keep her out of harm's way, and, despite her brave talk, he had doubts about her ability to defend herself.

He decided he'd just have to make the best of it.

"We're going to need some supplies…"

"Follow me. I know just where to go."

Chapter 5 – The Forest

Maximillion followed Katherine down to the barracks where the soldiers who were responsible for patrolling the river stayed. Katherine chose three strong horses from a corral full of trail-wise animals. They saddled two and packed the third with bedrolls, food,

and weapons; mounted; and rode toward The Forest. The gate that led out into The Forest was guarded, but Katherine simply waved to the guards and they were outside the walls of the city.

Maximillion shook his head, "I can't believe we got away without so much as a question."

"Few people will question you if you act as if you've a right to be where you are. I just hope the guards aren't punished."

"Well, we'll just have to get back with the powder before anyone knows we're gone."

They rode as far as the light would allow that night, camping only when they could no longer see the trail. They ate dried meat and bread soaked in water. Neither felt they could risk a fire so close to the city. Katherine was up before dawn. She had the horses saddled and jerky ready when Maximillion woke. They were on the trail as the sun rose.

They traveled for three days, surrounded by lush, green forest. There was no sign of pursuit from the city, and Maximillion began to relax. Should they be discovered, Katherine would be taken back to the castle with a slap on the wrist, but consequences would be much less pleasant for her traveling companion.

Soon, however, Maximillion had other matters to occupy his thoughts. The land was beginning to change. With each passing hour, the trail faded, the underbrush thickened, and The Forest darkened. He turned and looked behind him. The path was gone. Only The Forest remained.

A shudder passed down Maximillion's spine as he realized they were in the grasp of The Unknown.

Maximillion heard a soft, low piping coming from somewhere to his left. He had no idea from what direction it came: east, west, north, or south had no meaning here. He followed the sound and found a small man dressed all in green and brown perched on a tree stump.

The small man's mouth fell open in surprise, then he said, "Well, hello fellow travelers. Welcome! Welcome!" He gestured with his flute. "Sit with me and tell me your songs."

"My song?" asked Maximillion.

"The song of your life. From whence do you come and where do you go? What do you love and what do you hate? Tell me this and I will share with you a feast beyond a king's imagining."

Maximillion smiled and told his story of the smithy, how Katherine came to travel with him, The Stranger and his powder. Then it was Katherine's turn. She told of life in the castle, of her schooling and training, of her hopes and dreams for her people.

When it was done, the small man clapped and expressed appreciation. "Well told, my friends. Well told." He then took two bowls from his tattered brown rucksack and ladled some stew into them. A piece of stale bread served as a spoon. Maximillion took it with a grunt of gratitude and dived in. It was indeed a feast fit for a king.

"The Stranger you describe: I believe I may have seen him last full moon. He was on a pinky-patchy horse and his cuirass was shiny-bright."

Maximillion sat up straight. "Indeed, friend, that sounds like the man I seek. May I ask where you saw him?"

"Somewhere out there," said the piper, gesturing wide with his arms. "Keep the sound of water always on your left and you will find him."

The small man's offer of a sleeping place by the fire was gratefully accepted, but Maximillion had a hard time getting to sleep. He now had a real lead on The Stranger and was eager to get on the trail.

In the morning, Katherine was again ready to go as Maximillion was waking.

"I wish I had something to offer you, as thanks for your kindness," Katherine said as she shook the piper's hand.

"All I ask is to know the end of your song. It will help those not yet born to understand who Maximillion and Katherine were, help them understand the journey upon which you now embark. Perhaps one day we'll meet again and you will sing it for me. I know that before long you will create your own legend," he said with a smile.

They both promised to tell the wee man the end of their tale, thanked him again for his kindness, then sped on their way. Maximillion kept his host's words in mind and traveled so the river was always on their left.

The farther they went into the west, the more challenging became the terrain. The river seemed to bend gradually to the north. There were large boulders to skirt, chasms to traverse, and choking underbrush to hack through. Through it all, Katherine and Maximillion moved as one.

They had just made camp in a small clearing, three nights since meeting the wee piper, when they heard something crashing through the brush. Maximillion jumped up, rummaged in his rucksack for the short dagger, and had just found it when an ocelot bounded into the small clearing.

The cat pulled up short, surprised at finding humans in the dark woods.

Katherine calmed the horses, who had been frightened by the noise. Maximillion crouched and pointed the knife at the small cat, who promptly sat down and began licking his left paw.

"Shoo," commanded Maximillion, waving his weapon at the feline.

The cat gave him a withering look and began cleaning his ears.

"Git! Go on, scat!"

The cat stopped cleaning himself and looked Maximillion in the eye. "Why should I scat, pray tell? There seems to be room enough here for all of us."

Maximillion staggered backward and sat down heavily.

"You talk?"

"Apparently," said the cat, dryly. "I've come all this way to share important news with you, and you want me to scat."

Maximillion said nothing, but tried to accept the reality of a talking cat. Perhaps those berries he'd had earlier were not safe for eating after all.

Was this a vision? Was important information coming to him in the form of a hallucination? If so, he'd better take heed.

"What information, pray tell, noble cat?"

"Call me Desmond. So now I'm a *noble* cat! A moment ago you were waving a cutting tool in my face."

"I apologize for that. You startled me."

The cat paused, scratching a spot just above his left shoulder.

"Fair enough. You're forgiven." Desmond sniffed the air and his golden eyes widened, "Have you any food to offer a weary traveler?"

"Why, yes." Katherine dug a piece of dried meat out of their sack, pulled off a piece and threw it to Maximillion, who carefully offered it to the animal.

Desmond took the offering in his paw, sniffed it, and took a cautious bite.

"Rabbit? Not dried very well. Tastes a bit gamey."

Maximillion nodded agreement. "It's hard to dry meat properly when traveling. It's the best I have."

Desmond wiped his paw on a bit of moss. "Stops the rumbling, though, don't it? Thanks for sharing."

Maximillion cleared his throat. "You said you had important information for me?"

The cat nodded.

"Indeed."

Desmond jumped onto a large rock, puffed out his chest with importance, and looked down upon Maximillion. "I have seen him whom you seek."

"Who, The Stranger? How do you know whom I seek?"

Desmond ignored the interruption and continued. "Two days past, our paths crossed. He travels north, an old man on an old horse."

Two days! Maximillion couldn't possibly make camp now, not when The Stranger was so close. Katherine obviously had the same thought. She was readying the horses. They had to locate the man, find the secret to the silver powder, get back home, and get weapons made for the Prince's army.

"Thank you, noble Desmond," said Maximillion as he broke camp, "your news may well save my people and my country from destruction. Even now a great army masses, ready to march. They wait only for the waters of the great river to calm."

Maximillion threw the last of the dried rabbit to the cat. Desmond grabbed it in midair and hunkered down for a fine meal.

Maximillion and Katherine rode all night, keeping the sound of the river on their left. They paused now and again to listen for The Stranger: a snort, a horse stamping its hoof, anything that might give away the position of the scarred man.

The night passed away, then the next day, and night was again upon the weary travelers. They were bone tired, but dared not rest. The Warrior King could even now be marching on MidChester. Maximillion thought of his family, the gardens, and the world he knew. The thought of the armies of the Warrior King laying waste to his city was too terrible to think about. He must keep going, despite the hunger and pain and weariness.

Maximillion tightened his belt, hoping it would ease the complaining of his stomach. Their food was running low, and they had to conserve some for the trip back to MidChester. He wished now that he hadn't given Desmond the last of the dried rabbit, but it was too late for wishes, and he didn't want to waste time hunting. Katherine always had her bow cocked, but it was impossible to get a clear shot in this green maze. They'd just have to make the best of it.

His foot was stinging like fire, and Maximillion knew something was wrong. He sat down on a log next to a small brook and removed his boot. One of his many blisters, this one on his big toe, had broken and was bleeding. He dipped his foot in the water, hoping to ease the pain and clean the wound.

Katherine pulled a small medical kit from the pack and uncorked a jar of salve, applied some of the tarry substance to the blister, then slipped a piece of dry gut over Maximillion's toe.

"Thank you. That feels a lot better."

"You're welcome." Katherine ran an appraising eye over the brook. "Think there's any fish in there?"

It looked like a body of water that should have fish in it, but Maximillion saw none. If he caught one, he'd swallow it whole. He splashed water on his face, and his dry, cracked skin tightened in response. He felt desperation creeping into his mind and quickly brushed it aside. This was nothing. No one had ever died from a little blister and there would be time enough for food later.

Suddenly, they were surrounded by armed men. One threw a lasso around Maximillion's shoulders and pulled the young smithy to the ground, but his first thought was of the young princess.

"Katherine!'

"I'm all right."

The others laughed and searched his pack, throwing its contents hither and yon.

"I'm all right," one of the gang mocked.

"You won't be for long, sweetheart," another answered.

"Stale bread and dried fruit," said the one rummaging through the packs.

"You useless pup. We may as well cook and eat you."

"Hey, that aren't a half bad idea. I don't mind eating him."

"He seems pretty scrawny," a short, long-haired thug chimed in, a sour look on his seamed face. "Chewy."

"How 'bout her, then?"

Everyone looked at Katherine. Her eyes widened to the size of horseshoes and she struggled wildly against the ropes that bound her.

Maximillion swallowed hard. They were in real trouble.

Suddenly, arrows appeared in two of the outlaws' chests and they toppled to the ground. The other three made surprised noises and reached for their weapons. One was dead before his sword could clear its scabbard. Another was able to make one swing before the gleaming blade found a home in his belly. One turned tail and ran, but a dagger at the base of his skull cut short his bid for freedom.

The Stranger wiped his blade on the leader's shirt, then sheathed his blade.

"We meet again, young blacksmith."

Maximillion let out a sigh of relief and sank to the ground. They had been saved.

After Katherine introduced herself, The Stranger told Maximillion that he had been tracking this band of outlaws since he had come across the bodies of three of their victims two days past. Tattoos on all the men's arms attested to the fact they were deserters from the Warrior King's Army.

Maximillion shuddered. To think of thousands of men such as these loose in MidChester....

He quickly told The Stranger of the Warrior King's massing army and their quest for more powder to create stronger armor to defend the city.

"My camp is just over the next rise. Tonight, you two need to rest and eat. Tomorrow, we have much to do."

They gathered their scattered belongings and led the horses to The Stranger's camp, where the patchy horse and a pack animal whinnied hello to the new arrivals. The Stranger broke out his formidable supply of food and told Maximillion and Katherine to help themselves. Maximillion's mouth was watering when he saw the bounty the leather sack contained. Katherine pulled out some dried meat and vegetables, gathered water from the stream, and set about creating a meal.

The Stranger had been very quiet after hearing Maximillion tell of the impending invasion by the Warrior King, but once they reached camp, it was his turn to tell his story to Maximillion and Katherine. He explained that he was quite familiar with the Warrior King, for it was his soldiers who had lain waste to the lands of his people so many years ago. The Stranger had been a young man then, and he had set out on the same quest that Maximillion was now on.

The Stranger told Maximillion that his people had learned to fashion armor from the scales of The Dragon that lived up the side of the mountains to the north, beyond The Forest. These scales could be found deep in the caves where The Dragon nested. Many men had died trying to collect the scales, for The Dragon guarded his cave well.

By the time The Stranger's lands were invaded by The Warrior King, his people had been living in peace for many years and had abandoned their defenses, armor, and weaponry. When they learned of the impending invasion, The Stranger was chosen to lead a party up into the mountains to collect the scales of The Dragon.

The expedition did not fare well. When they attempted to enter the caves, they found The Dragon awake, alert, and angry at the intrusion. Any sane person would simply have fled, but their situation was desperate. The Warrior King's Army was approaching and there was no choice. They must battle The Dragon for its scales.

Their armor still could not protect the group from the fire-breathing lizard. One by one the men fell to the creature's deadly breath. In desperation, The Stranger swung his sword at the beast and landed a glancing blow just over The Dragon's heart, shearing off several silvery scales as his sword shattered and flew across the floor.

The Stranger grabbed the scales as The Dragon fanned his searing breath across the cavern, charring the flesh off the young boy's face. The last of his men were killed drawing The Dragon away so that The Stranger could escape.

The Stranger limped home with his precious cargo, but by the time he returned to his city, all was in ruin, his people annihilated. And there were too few scales to make more than his own armor and sword. The Stranger created the sword, Silverthorne, as a tribute to his people and their fate.

Wracked with guilt and loneliness, he spent years wandering alone in The Forest.

Maximillion, Katherine, and The Stranger sat in silence in the glowing light of the camp fire. It was The Stranger who spoke first.

"You now face the same challenge I faced years ago. I will go with you into the lair. I have unfinished business with both The Dragon and the Warrior King."

The Stranger went to his pack and pulled out a rolled skin. "This is a map that my father made of this forest and the path to The Dragon's cave. No sense stumbling around blindly if we can take advantage of his hard work."

"I believe we're here," said The Stranger, pointing to a place on the map where a large boulder caused the river to fork.

Maximillion and Katherine both agreed. They could see the boulder, which was more the size of a small, gray mountain, from where they camped.

"And the lair of the great Dragon is here." He tapped his finger on a sooty imprint not far from the base of the formidable mountains whose peaks they had been seeing off in the distance.

"Is it far?" asked Katherine.

"We'll be at the base of the mountain by tomorrow evening. Won't take long if you're not wasting time by hacking through every thicket you come across." The Stranger smiled at the dismayed looks on his two friends' faces. "Here, let me show you a fast way back to the city." The three hunkered over the map, The Stranger showing them in great detail how to find the path back to MidChester.

"The map's a wonderful help," said Maximillion as he settled down with a warm cup of tea and fresh biscuit, "We'd never be able to keep to the trail without it. The map shows all the signs to look for along the way."

"Yes, thank you so much for your guidance," Katherine said as she delivered a plate of stew to The Stranger.

"My father spent years creating this map of The Forest," said The Stranger, "and he explained its ins and outs to me before he died. I want you to take the map," he said, handing it to Maximillion, "so that your people need never again wonder how to navigate The Forest. Instead of a great Unknown, it will be a friendly place where one can find shelter, sustenance, and wealth. Your craftsmen can copy this map and distribute it to the people. My father's handiwork can be used to allay the fears of your people."

The three travelers set off again the next day, venturing still farther north. With The Stranger's map, they were able to keep to a fairly well-defined path, although it was challenging to spot for the uninitiated, and they covered ground quickly. Late afternoon found them in the foothills, and by the time the sun set, they had set up camp at the base of a great range of mountains. A sheer rock wall rose several hundred feet in front of them, and above the plateau soared a massive peak whose summit was lost in a misty haze.

"We'll camp here tonight," The Stranger instructed. "We'll eat well. Make sure we're in good shape for the climb tomorrow."

They ate from The Stranger's stores again. It was a cold meal of bread and dried meat, both soaked in water to soften them, dried fruit and nuts. Maximillion longed for some fresh meat, but he knew they couldn't risk a fire so close to The Dragon's lair. After eating, they talked for a bit, then all three fell asleep.

Chapter 6 – The Dragon

In the morning they woke, well rested and with fresh minds. They had a light breakfast of dried fish and fruit, and drank from the clear stream that issued from the cliff. They made sure the horses were safe and secure, for who knew how long they would be up the mountain, or if they would ever return.

Finally, when the camp and animals were secure, the three looked at each other. There was no other work left but the climb.

"Well, let's be about it." Maximillion said.

So they climbed, the three of them. They scratched and clawed their way up the cliff face, making as little noise as possible. Maximillion's hands and feet ached with the effort of climbing. His muscles were screaming for him to stop and rest. But there was no rest here on the cliff face.

The sun beat down relentlessly upon them. Maximillion was able to sneak a look at Katherine who was climbing to his right. She was concentrating hard, and her face was pink from exertion, but she looked exhilarated. What would they find above in the lair? Was The

Dragon still alive? If it were, would they be able to kill it and harvest its scales?

So many questions assailed Maximillion. He had to push them from his mind and concentrate on the climb. The climb was all that mattered now. One foot in front of the other, find the next handhold and swing up. The Stranger led the way, making sure his sword didn't bang against the rock and give away their position.

With silent celebration, the exhausted trio crested the sheer cliff and arrived upon the plateau. They rested for a while and refreshed themselves with water from a nearby creek and dried apples from The Stranger's pack. They rested until their hearts no longer pounded and their limbs no longer trembled from the effort. Then, The Stranger rose wordlessly, adjusted his armor and sword, and approached the black spot in the mountain where the beast dwelt.

As they neared the cave, a stench worse than any abattoir assaulted their nostrils. Something about the smell struck an ancient fear within Maximillion, and he felt a terror more profound than any he had ever known. They entered the cave, pressing themselves flat against the right wall. A few feet inside the mouth and the sunlight was gone. They paused, letting their eyes adjust to the darkness. Throwing off his cloak and drawing Silverthorne, The Stranger's faintly glowing armor and sword shed just enough light to allow them to creep forward.

The cave floor was littered with animal carcasses, many of them recent kills. As they moved deeper into the cavern, they discovered the fate of those adventurers who had traveled deep into The Forest, never to be heard from again. Human bones, broken blades, and armor littered the floor of the cave. Maximillion looked at Katherine, who was visibly shaken.

Suddenly, the entire cave wall to their far left seemed to shift and rise up. Huge blood-red eyes glared at them from the darkness. The Stranger shoved Maximillion and Katherine behind him. With a fierce cry, he charged The Dragon, swinging Silverthorne, the blade made from The Dragon's own scales.

His attack caught The Dragon by surprise. It reared up as The Stranger's blade slashed deep into its shoulder.

Maximillion pressed himself harder against the wall, trying to shield Katherine as best he could. With no armor and only the small dagger, he knew how a field mouse must feel when facing a hawk. Maximillion swallowed, steeled himself, and prepared to circle around to The Dragon's flank. The Stranger was in trouble and Maximillion and Katherine had to figure out a way to save him. As Katherine moved into position, looking for a clear shot as she drew back her bow, Maximillion circled to the left.

Maximillion reached The Dragon's far side just in time to see The Stranger strike another blow against The Dragon's injured limb. The creature roared in pain and surprise, knocking The Stranger across the cavern with one swipe of its powerful tail.

Maximillion saw Katherine take aim with her bow. She fired at the dragon's shoulder, but her arrow bounced off the heavy plating of the injured lizard. She notched another arrow and let it fly. This one sank deep within the gash created by Silverthorne.

The Dragon writhed in pain, snaking this way and that, its injured arm curled against its chest. Maximillion searched desperately for a place to shelter from the great lizard's wrath. The creature writhed back and forth. It crashed into the walls and struck the ceiling, and then Maximillion found himself staring at The Dragon's chest. As he gasped for what he thought were certainly the last breaths of his life, he saw the scar over The Dragon's heart where, years ago, a young man not unlike himself had sheared off The Dragon's scales.

With all the strength that he could bring to bear, Maximillion drove his dagger deep into the beast's evil heart. The Dragon let loose an unholy scream as it reared up high, then collapsed in a lifeless heap on the cavern floor.

Maximillion ran to The Stranger, who lay crumpled against the wall of the cave. He was bleeding badly, his breath rapid and shallow.

"Is, is it dead?"

"Yes! It will trouble these lands no more."

The Stranger coughed up an alarming amount of blood. "Then my people are avenged."

Katherine knelt beside the injured man, trying to stem the flow of blood, to no avail.

"Take this," the Stranger said pushing Silverthorne into Maximillion's hands. "It will be up to you now to ensure that the Warrior King suffers a similar fate." And with that, the Stranger was gone.

Maximillion and Katherine buried their friend beside The Dragon. On a stone, Maximillion etched, "Here Lies a DragonSlayer," and he placed the stone on the ground in front of the Dragon's open jaws.

He fashioned a marker by driving an old pike into the ground and draping the Stranger's cloak over it.

Maximillion knew he had no time for grief. He was no longer sure how much time had passed since he had left his home city. He had no way of knowing whether the Warrior King's Army had reached the river. He only knew he had to pack onto the horses as many of The Dragon's scales as they could carry.

They rode to the south and east at a relentless pace, following The Stranger's map and instructions. Again, the path was easy to find when they knew what to look for. They approached the city after two nights of hard riding.

The horses were nearly dead from exhaustion as Maximillion and Katherine emerged from The Forest on the western side of the city. In the distance, they could see the Warrior King's siege towers rolling in from the east. The King's Army was massing on the bank of the great river, working to destroy the bridge before anyone could cross.

Chapter 7 – The Return

The King's guards hardly recognized Maximillion, for now he was clad in The Stranger's glowing silver armor and carried Silverthorne at his side. They recognized Katherine, though, and word quickly spread throughout the town that the missing princess had returned with a handsome warrior at her side.

Maximillion told the guards that he needed an urgent audience with the Prince. He told one of the guards to take the horses immediately to his father's blacksmith shop and wait for him there. Surprised by the authority in Maximillion's voice, the soldiers responded without question.

Maximillion was taken before the Prince and told his tale as briefly as possible. He explained to the Prince that he would need to have the authority to take charge of the Guild if they were to work together to fashion enough armor and weaponry to equip the King's Army.

Having little to lose, given the sight of the vast numbers of the Warrior King's Army, the Prince granted Maximillion the authority to take charge of the Guild.

Katherine pulled Maximillion aside. "I'm needed here, with the troops. I'll help prepare them, let them know that you're creating invincible armor that will defeat the Warrior King's Army."

Maximillion knew she was right, but hated to be separated from her. "I'll see you soon." He kissed her, which surprised Maximillion as much as it did Katherine.

As Maximillion rushed back to his father's shop, he dispatched soldiers to summon each of the other shop owners who were part of the Blacksmiths' Guild.

Like a general, Maximillion began organizing his "troops" into teams. Maximillion quickly showed one team how to grind the scales into powder. Then, he taught the blacksmiths how to combine the powder with earth and fresh water to create the new metal.

Rather than the tradespeople from each shop working individually on one piece of armor, Maximillion arranged them into teams along long benches. Each team was assigned a component of the process needed to complete a suit of armor. One smith created plates of metal, another banged it into shape, and yet another smith welded the pieces together to create the armor's chest plate. With five such teams in operation, the armor was quickly produced.

He directed the smiths of his father's shop to concentrate on making swords and set them up in teams. One man mixed the powder, earth, and water to create the metal. Another gave a rough shape to the sword, one man honed the weapon, and the last smith tempered the blade. In all, Maximillion was able to organize six teams of sword makers.

Another shop was to focus on arrowheads, and the last shop was to fashion the shafts for the arrowheads. These two shops were arranged in teams also. Soon, there was no need for Maximillion's direction. The shop owners were directing their own men at their appointed tasks.

In the days that it took the Warrior King to amass his army on the banks of the great river, Maximillion's "army" of craftsmen had produced enough armor and weaponry to equip every soldier in the Prince's regiment. They were still outnumbered easily ten to one, but they were now equipped with superior technology.

As the Warrior King's soldiers began crossing the river, they found themselves showered with arrows that pierced their armor plating. As they scaled the walls on their siege towers, they were met with swords that cut right through their own swords and armor.

After three days of fierce fighting, the Warrior King's forces retreated back across the river and back to the east.

Maximillion thought of The Stranger as he watched the army retreat. He knew this victory would not have been possible without him. The Stranger had made certain that the people of MidChester would have a far different fate than his. Holding Silverthorne in his hand Maximillion realized that he was a DragonSlayer.

The Prince summoned Maximillion to the castle where, with much pomp and ceremony, he was granted a noble title, given land and treasure.

As a noble, he was now free to ask for Katherine's hand in marriage.

They were married in the gardens, in front of the fountain where they had planned their foray into The Forest.

Over the years, they had three children, who quickly grew to eight, thirteen, and eighteen. And it was the thirteen year old who was always focused on new technology. Maximillion laughed as he heard his father's voice coming out of his own mouth, telling his son, "Come over here and focus!"

Maximillion remained involved in the Guild and had taken over his father's smithy, which now specialized in short swords and daggers. He also helped other business owners specialize in niche markets and take advantage of their strong points. He pioneered new techniques in blacksmithing and was widely renowned for his craftsmanship and innovation.

Life was good, though Maximillion longed for more time with his family. He'd become an expert craftsman, and his time was always in great demand. He'd built the smithy into a prosperous business, and like his father before him, he was always at the center. He was the hub of a great wheel which seemed to be turning ever a bit faster.

From the day of his marriage, Maximillion assumed that he would live happily ever after....

Or not...

Section II – Max's Dilemma

Chapter 8 – The Jungle

It was dark. Darker than it seemed it should be to Maximillion as he exited the door of the smithy and looked up at the high stone walls of the city. At the edges of his shadowy perception, he sensed something hanging down over the top of the wall, encroaching: Vines – a cascade of strange vines was hanging down over the top of the wall.

Maximillion walked down the cobblestone street. It was completely silent. Not a soul in sight as he approached the city gates and walked out toward The Forest. Where were the guards?

Everything seemed wrong – the wrong sounds, the wrong smells. Everything felt unfamiliar.

Maximillion realized he was surrounded by the thick tangle – The Forest had been transformed into The Jungle. Encased in armor, the heat felt unbearable to Maximillion. Glowing eyes were all around. Strange and dangerous animals seemed to be closing in.

He looked down at his sword and his armor, and he felt utterly ill-equipped for this… the vines encircling him, a tangled mass, making him feel… trapped!

At 5:30 a.m. on the dot, Max woke before the alarm clock even went off. He heard the distant beeping sound of his automatic drip coffee maker downstairs in the kitchen. He felt far too tired to get out of bed, and yet the aroma of the coffee came drifting up the stairs, calling to him.

Max sat up on the edge of his bed and rubbed his eyes. "Happily every after" indeed! Where the hell had that dream come from? And yet he instantly related to that last scene. Lost in a jungle, filled with dangerous viruses and predators, with the wrong tools. Tools that were perfect for dealing with forests, dragons, and invading medieval warlords, but that were totally inadequate for dealing with an encroaching jungle.

Good luck hacking through tangled vines with a broad sword! Why did that image make him feel cranky all of a sudden?

At 47, Max had built his law practice to include two junior partners. But 80 hours a week for how many years now? Why did all the fairy tales end with "happily ever after" right at the point where real life started accelerating to a pace that felt just shy of out-of-control?

Why did all the fairy tales end with "happily ever after" right at the point where real life started accelerating to a pace that felt just shy of out-of-control?

As he shuffled down the stairs, his half-asleep mind following his nose, he reflected on the image of the journey through the forest, slaying the dragon to acquire something special that would take him to the top. Wasn't that what all those years of college, law school, and clerkship were all about? In some romantic way, back then he'd felt like a conquering hero when he finally placed that framed JD degree on his wall. *Unstoppable*, that's how he had felt then. How long ago now?

And while he was not quite willing to equate the larger firms in town with invading warlords, the image did please him just a little bit.

Max's musings were disrupted just then as his 13-year-old daughter came flying into the room, laptop over her shoulder, texting a message on her Blackberry with a single hand while grabbing the milk out of the fridge with the other. For just a moment, Max had a flash to one of those Star Trek episodes with the Borg – half human, half machine, and fully integrated into a collective network.

Was it actually possible to have a conversation with his daughter without feeling like hundreds (or was it thousands now?) of others were in the loop on Facebook and Twitter? He shook his head, thinking that he was just a little behind this part of the technology curve. "Digital life versus analog life" was a phrase that suddenly popped into his mind. Online and offline life were a seamless transition for her. It was the water through which she swam – effortlessly.

It was not that he disliked the online world. Far from it. For example, he'd become an addict when it came to the Kona coffee that he ordered online every couple of weeks right from Killino's Farm in Hawaii. It pleased him to think how accessible everything had become on the Internet.

Every couple of weeks, Max logged in, placed his order, and that very day someone thousands of miles away was putting coffee beans into a roaster, sealing them in a bag, and mailing them off to him. In about three days' time he had a couple of pounds of dark, delicious beans right off the side of a Hawaiian volcano. "Are there jungles in Hawaii?" Max muttered as he poured a cup to take up to his wife, Kate.

He thought about The Jungle again, re-imagining the scene. It wasn't that he lacked *any* of the right tools. As he drank down the last of his first cup of Kona, he saw himself in a khaki explorer's outfit with the silly helmet and a machete. Dressed and equipped, but just aimlessly hacking away at the jungle with no real impact.

He was lost because what was intuitively obvious to his 13-year-old daughter was often a confusing mystery to him. As he poured his second cup and headed off for the shower, he grumbled to himself, "No maps..." No maps and no time to explore The Jungle.

It had all seemed easier when there *were* dragons to slay. There was a structure and a sequence to follow. There was a curriculum. And there was that feeling that with each challenge overcome, he was scaling to new heights. The path had seemed clear back then. But now?

Now, he just kept working harder and faster. Those vines were encroaching, tangling around his feet, threatening to bog everything down and choke the life out of... Out of what? Out of him, out of his business... out of his life's satisfaction? Maybe all of the above.

As he headed out the door 30 minutes later, Max thought about his daughter and Kate just a couple of months back. Until then, his wife had resisted setting up a profile on Facebook because she was concerned that some of her clients might try to "Friend" her, creating some awkward dynamics in her psychotherapy practice. Boundaries were important, and the social rules of this online world were still pretty murky.

But after getting an email from their oldest son who was away at college, Kate's reluctance had eased. She had asked him about the lack of response to her last email. He then explained to her that no one used email anymore and she really needed to get on Facebook if she were going to stay connected with his generation. That and she might consider getting the hang of texting!

She was sitting with their daughter that night, and in minutes, clicking away on the laptop, their daughter had set up a complete profile for Kate. No thought, no effort – it was amazing to watch.

Stuck in traffic, Max began to feel the frustration-level building yet again. It wasn't the traffic making him grip the wheel so hard. He realized that he was probably in the midst of a total mid-life crisis. He was tired all the time, his income had plateaued a while back, and it just felt like everything was shifting all around him at a pace that did not permit him the time to adapt.

Max hit the horn even though he realized it was pointless. The treadmill of his life was moving so fast that he often thought he would fly off the back if he even tried to catch his breath. Just shy of out-of-control, he thought again.

He wasn't sleeping well. He kept having these weird dreams about the blacksmith and dragons and invading armies. He didn't have time for fairy tales. No Stranger was showing up with a pouch of magic powder to solve his problems! What he needed was sleep. That and a good long vacation – time to think.

If he could simply find a way to take the last twenty years of professional knowledge and experience he had acquired and put it into his 13-year-old daughter's head, he could then give her the job of marketing his practice.

If he could simply find a way to take the last twenty years of professional knowledge and experience he had acquired and put it into his 13-year-old daughter's head, he could then give her the job of marketing his practice. In this crazy, cold, impersonal Online Jungle, he was not only facing it – but feeling lost in it as well! Or if he could find a way to absorb the ease with which she "saw" the world in terms of integrated networks, then maybe he could find a way to move his skill, expertise, and experience through those networks effectively.

On the one hand, Max was at the top of his game. He commanded a very respectable hourly rate for his services. On the other hand, he had hit this plateau for that very reason. He provided a service and billed by the hour. So, how was he supposed to grow and develop from here?

There were no more hours that he could put in if he wanted to survive past the age of 50. His father had died in his early sixties from a massive heart attack. Max knew in his own heart, quite literally, that he could not continue down this path. Something had to give or it would be his health giving out first.

He already saw the warning signs. There were a few extra pounds piling up around his midsection because there was no time for exercise. His diet was less than perfect because there was either no time to eat, or it was the never-ending crunch-time that caused him to grab junk on the fly. You'd think that being trapped on this *treadmill* of life would at least keep you in shape!

Max thought about a conversation he'd recently had with one of the junior partners about Tim Ferriss' book **The 4-Hour Workweek**. Now how crazy was that? Here was a guy writing about working fewer hours to make more money. Somehow Max had missed out on the memo about the ultimate money-making system that was going to make that happen! He laughed a bit bitterly when he realized that he did not even have the time in his schedule to *contemplate* reading the book.

The only way Max could conceive of growing his business was to look for one more good client and/or to find a client who could afford to pay him more an hour. The only way the firm grew was to take on additional associates, creating a larger client base. But with each expansion, the overhead grew in proportion as well, making it hard to feel they were ever really getting ahead. Besides, the added stress of a larger operation hardly seemed to justify the small expansion in revenue.

There was a side to all of this that made Max feel he was missing the point in some fundamental sense. He just wasn't quite clear what that point was. By any stretch of the imagination, he was a successful person. He had gone to college and done well. He had gone to law school and done well. His career had progressed to the point that he was the managing partner of his firm and he knew that this frustration he was feeling was not really about money, per se.

Still, he felt trapped. He felt that he had clearly hit a plateau. The lack of income growth was just the most obvious *symbol* of that plateau. There was nowhere else to go from here. There was no more room for real advancement. From here on out, it was all more of the same.

Kate saw his growing frustration and was trying not to push too hard to have him go see one of her colleagues for some stress-reduction therapy. She was just waiting for him to show up in the driveway with a bright red convertible or some other form of materialistic candy to make himself feel young and alive again. Frankly, that little red car sounded pretty good to her, too. But Max was smart enough to know that he wanted more than a band-aid to take the edge off. There had to be a better way; he just had no idea what that was.

And that's what was so confusing to him. This was the *bullseye* on the target of his career. He had arrived exactly where all the years of training and hard work had been aimed at getting him. This was supposed to *be* the summit. And now here he was, stuck on this plateau!

He had arrived exactly where all the years of training and hard work had been aimed at getting him. This was supposed to be the summit. And now here he was, stuck on this plateau!

Only now did he realize that all his effort had gone into achieving this goal, but almost no thought had gone into defining what the longer term goal really was, what it all really *meant*.

"There's not a whole lot of here, here," he thought to himself.

Chapter 9 – Lost

A few hours later, as Max sat in his office preparing to head out for this quarter's meeting with his accountant, he felt a bit ungrateful as he looked around and asked, "Is this it? Is this all there is?" But he simply could not deny how he *felt*.

He felt that he had set out on a mission to reach a summit, but somehow he had followed the flawed map he'd been given.

This did not feel like a peak experience. He did not have some deep feeling of contentment and satisfaction. Just the opposite. He felt like a caged animal. He felt that he had set out on a mission to reach a summit, but somehow he had followed the flawed map he'd been given.

That was the problem. If success were equal to money, then life should be great. And that seemed to be the map that everyone was using. Success came with a nice house, a nice car, and maybe two weeks off – staying in touch with the office by phone and email on a daily basis, of course. That plan also happened to come with a boat-load of bills that just kept the cycle churning. High income, high debt, and no free time.

But, if in getting the money you had to give away all of your time, then how could you ever consider yourself wealthy?

Suddenly, Max found his mind drifting back to the blacksmith in his dream. It took *time* to live "happily ever after." *Ever after* was a measurement of time, not of money. That was important, but Max was not quite sure what to do with it.

> **It took time to live "happily ever after." Ever after was a measurement of time, not of money.**

When was the last real vacation they had been able to take, Max wondered. The kind where you actually had time to feel bored, the kind where you could actually turn off the smart-phone, the kind where no one could find you? Being lost in the jungle had some appeal, come to think of it!

But if taking time back costs you the money, how was that going to work out? He had one son in college already and another two kids in the pipeline. Those were bills that were not going to pay themselves. His dad had found a pretty slick way – work until you literally drop dead. Then you can finance your family's needs with life insurance!

His mind was way off on a tangent at this point. But insurance seemed like such a strange concept. The more that he thought about it just then, the stranger it seemed. There was no time to eat right and exercise. So, rather than trying to have good health, rather than having a really great life, we buy insurance to cover the value of the life we're not really living.

Now fully confident that he was losing it, he pushed this line of thinking even further.

Okay, so now we are not only working hard to pay the bills, we are adding new bills for life and disability and health insurance, thus requiring that we work more hours to cover the premiums for the insurance that is needed to cover the expenses that will arise as a result of no longer being able to work to pay the bills and pay for that insurance because we have just dropped dead!

His head was spinning.

"Okay, sure, now *that* makes total sense," Max muttered, causing some of the office staff to glance over at him nervously. So by dropping dead like his father, Max could provide his family with the means of having some time without having to work to pay the mortgage, the car payments, and the college tuition bills. It was all getting pretty clear now!

And then an even darker thought crept into Max's mind. What if his father hadn't dropped dead of a heart attack, but instead had been severely disabled. Life insurance seemed like a better deal than trying to live on the 60 percent income that might come from a disability insurance policy. If you even had disability insurance.

Max sat at his desk with his head between his hands. His head hurt from that last train of thought. He looked up and stared out the window for a few minutes watching traffic go by. What was wrong with him? Was everyone out there running so fast in a circle that they had dug a moat around themselves, too? Max was aware of both a heaviness and a tightness across his chest.

Was everyone out there running so fast in a circle that they had dug a moat around themselves, too?

His body knew that there was something very wrong about all of this.

One thing seemed clear to Max. He realized that he was lost. Acknowledging the problem is the first step to finding a solution, right? And he realized that he was going to need a much better map. He just had no clue where that might be found.

In that moment, he remembered something that he had read and saved several years earlier. It was called **Lost**. He did a quick search and pulled it up on his computer.

Lost[1]

Stand still. The trees ahead and the bushes beside you
Are not lost. Wherever you are is called Here,
And you must treat it as a powerful stranger,
Must ask permission to know it and be known.
The forest breathes. Listen. It answers,
I have made this place around you,
If you leave it you may come back again, saying Here.

No two trees are the same to Raven.
No two branches are the same to Wren.
If what a tree or a bush does is lost on you,
You are surely lost. Stand still. The forest knows
Where you are. You must let it find you.

"The forest knows where you are..." Max repeated. The Online Jungle probably knows where you are, too. Google was proof enough of that.

---

[1] Native American elder story rendered into modern English by David Wagoner in David Whythe, **The Heart Aroused – Poetry and the Preservation of the Soul in Corporate America**, Currency Doubleday, New York, 1996, p.259

To prove his point, Max typed his own name into the search engine to see what he might find. He noticed how his LinkedIn profile, the practice's website, and a few other links to information about him popped up. "You must let it find you," Max repeated, knowing that this was something important.

"Great, so if you already know who I am, you can find me online," Max muttered at the screen.

Clearly, the Online Jungle knew where he was. But beyond simply *being* here, he was unsure how to put this massive, tangled network to *work* for him. How was this supposed to help him get off this plateau?

...he was unsure how to put this massive, tangled network to work for him.

Max continued staring at the screen. He just had some far-away sense that there were answers here. They were somehow hidden from him. The blacksmith came back into his head. "Where do I find my Stranger who can reveal a little something special for me?"

The firm had hired consultants in the past to build each of these pieces for the business, like the website and the profiles on LinkedIn and Facebook. But there was no system tying the pieces together… no map. They just sat there. They did not *do* anything. He had to admit that he and his staff often made marketing decisions by looking at what everyone else in his profession did.

He had to admit that he and his staff often made marketing decisions by looking at what everyone else in his profession did.

You have to have a website in the same way you have to have a business card, right? But it was very clear to Max that their website was not even as good as his business card. He could hand his card to someone new when they met for the first time. But the only people who were coming to the website were people who already knew his firm.

His website was just where people could get a little background, a little more information. How was he supposed to make it *do* something pro-active? How was the website going to reach out to people and hand out his virtual business cards for him?

And with that thought, Max packed up the past quarter's numbers and headed out to meet with his accountant.

Chapter 10 – Max's Dilemma Revealed

Max and his accountant had been working together for years. After she finished printing out the current balance sheet and P&L reports, Max asked, "Allison, you've got a fair number of clients our age, right?"

"Sure."

"Well, have any of them figured it out?"

"Figured what out?" she asked with one eyebrow raised.

Sitting here thinking while Allison had been crunching numbers, Max's dilemma had become crystal clear to him. The choice always seemed to be between time or money. The dilemma was that by choosing more of one, you automatically

...Max's dilemma had become crystal clear to him. The choice always seemed to be between time or money.

decreased the other. It was a zero sum game. The solution always seemed simple, too: work more hours to increase your income while charging as much per hour as the market will bear.

Max shared these observations with Allison who pushed her chair away from her desk, leaned back, and looked up at the ceiling for a little while.

"You know Dr. Janet Brown, right? The pediatrician across town? A multi-million dollar operation but she has multi-million dollar overhead and insurance reimbursement rates going negative each year about as much as inflation is going up each year. And we won't even start to talk about malpractice rates in this state."

Allison got quiet again.

"You know," Allison continued after a pause, "I'm thinking of another fellow, too. A chiropractor. Just hit 63 this past year. As we sat down and went through his return this past year, we got to talking about retirement."

...his practice isn't really worth a dime without him. He is the entire business.

She went on, "He was saying that he didn't want to end up like some of his own patients who retire just in time to get laid up with something nasty and have no time to enjoy life. But the thing is: his practice isn't really worth a dime without him. *He* is the entire business. Believe me, I'm not giving away any of his secrets, he tells everybody that."

Allison shook her head, "Sure, he's got some equipment to sell off. But he never found a way to build real *value* into his business independent of his actual time. And, like a whole lot of us, what he socked away over the years got hammered as the market went south. Let me tell you, it was not a real cheerful conversation!"

Max was feeling less hopeful by the minute. He'd been looking to Allison for some stories of inspiration. So, no, this was not turning out to be all that cheerful a conversation either. Max wished he could just blame her!

"Well, surely you must know someone who's doing a better job of it," Max pressed.

"Yeah, well you know if you have products to sell in your business or you have patents and things with tangible value, it's a different story. But you and I chose the path of service. And what you're talking about right now is the real downside of this type of business. How's your singing voice? You could always record a hit single and live off royalties."

"Not with this voice!" Max picked it up from there. "You know, these things never even crossed my mind in the past. It's not like anyone sits you down in grad school and maps out the whole lifespan of your career for you. You go where your interests lead you."

It's not like anyone sits you down in grad school and maps out the whole lifespan of your career for you. You go where your interests lead you.

They fell silent for a long moment, then Max continued, "Looking back, it just seems like there should have been at least one class in the curriculum that talked about the *business* of the profession you're going into. But, no… nothing. It's like all those who have come before you have just pretended that this stuff magically gets figured out along the way!"

Allison chimed back in, "You know, I do have a colleague that I see a couple of times a year at meetings. What he did with his accounting practice was start developing software solutions for some targeted areas that solved problems for some of his clients."

She went on. "He was working with a lot of real estate investors and they would often struggle to crunch the numbers when trying to figure out what was or was not a really good deal. So he basically worked out all of the key ratios on a spreadsheet, hired someone to make it look pretty, and now he generates more income from the software than he does from his practice. Pretty sweet, actually," she said with a little envy in her tone.

After a moment's further reflection, Allison shared, "You know, I shouldn't really say anything. I'm in exactly the same boat you're in! If I stop crunching numbers and processing returns, where will I be?"

Max responded, "Yeah, well not a lot of my clients are looking for software for their legal problems." He was starting to feel frustrated again and figured it was probably time to get going before he got even more cranky. If this conversation went on any longer it was going to end up around the corner with a few martinis to take the edge off.

"Well, Allison, if someone tosses you a leather pouch with silvery powder, will you be sure to let me know? Maybe there's a dragon out there for us to bag."

Allison looked at him blankly. "Never mind," said Max. "You had to be there."

On the drive back to the office, Max thought about Allison's chiropractor client heading toward retirement. Max realized that, other than his partners buying out his share of the practice, his business had no real inherent value to anyone else. Certainly not to anyone outside the partnership.

He and his partners were the core of the business. They were the only thing producing income through hourly billing. What they sold was time... *their* time. And because they kept selling all their time, there was none left for them!

So how do I monetize that and sell it independent of just trading my time for money?

"So how do I monetize that and sell it independent of just trading my time for money?" he asked aloud to the traffic in front of him.

Max was beginning to understand that this dilemma was created by his mindset. His training had conditioned him to approach his business and model it based upon what everyone else in his profession was doing. Because he had built a business with himself at the center, and because he had built the kind of service business where what he was selling was his time, it was he who had created the problem.

There were no more hours in the week that he was willing to sell off. In fact, he was pretty willing to buy a few of them back if he could figure out how. He needed to own his time and find something else to sell.

And now the pace of change and the pace of life had brought this problem to the point of crisis. There were no more hours in the week that he was willing to sell off. In fact, he was pretty willing to buy a few of them back if he could figure out how. He needed to *own* his time and find something else to sell. He remembered someone once saying that on your deathbed, it's rarely more time in the office that you wish for. And Max didn't want that deathbed to come too quickly.

Chapter 11 – A New Direction

That night, over their usual late night dinner, Max discussed some of the day's events with Kate, and she told him about some of the challenges she was facing in her practice.

While she loved her work as a psychologist, she had to admit that she was most definitely in the same bind. There were only so many clients she was going to work with over any given week. There was a definite limit after which burnout became a really significant risk.

Max's daughter, who had been overhearing their conversation, started clicking away into Google on her laptop. She searched some of her parent's complaints, about being stuck on a plateau at mid-career, and about discovering the trap created by trading time for money, as well as all their frustrations about successfully marketing online as professionals.

After trying out some different combinations in Google's search window, she came over and said, "Dad, give me your iPhone for a minute, ok?"

She synched the phone to her laptop and after a few minutes handed it back to Max.

"Okay, Dad. Here's a playlist for you for the ride in to work."

"Thanks, Sweetheart..." Max smiled at his daughter, "I really appreciate it, but I don't think some better tunes are going to change things a whole lot."

"It's not music, Dad," she said rolling her eyes. "Give me a little credit. I subscribed you to a series of podcasts that sounds like pretty much exactly what you and Mom are talking about right now. Just check it out."

***

At exactly 5:30 am the next morning, the whole ritual began anew. As Max's feet hit the floor and he sat rubbing his eyes again, he realized that he could not recall anything he might have dreamt that night. Still he found himself thinking of some of the vivid images from the night before as he headed for his brain-refueling at the coffee machine.

He thought about the blacksmith heading off to slay the dragon. That seemed to him to represent his own journey of going off into the unknown, getting his professional training and degree. What struck him in that moment was something that at first had seemed like a completely trivial detail in the story.

As Maximillion and his companions had prepared to climb up to The Dragon's lair, there was a moment where he had glimpsed the summit of the Dragon's mountain.

As Maximillion and his companions had prepared to climb up to The Dragon's lair, there was a moment where he had glimpsed the summit of the Dragon's mountain.

What was it about that image, Max wondered as the caffeine started to rouse his worn neurons? In the dream, Maximillion did not have time to go for the summit. It was not even there as a conscious goal. There were more urgent matters. He had to get back to his city and save the day.

And Max thought about the journey of his own life. Slaying the professional dragon had led to building a business, raising a family, funding college tuition. Okay, it was not nearly as dramatic as driving out the Warrior King, but it was still the important stuff of life.

But what really struck Max was that image. Maximillion had seen a glimpse of the summit above the Dragon's lair, but it had barely registered. He needed to deal with the more pressing matters of the day. So it just barely entered his awareness, like some kind of subliminal message.

In the same way, Max's bigger dreams were set aside because his life had to focus on the practical. He had built his business and helped raise his family. But now, from Max's perspective at mid-career and mid-life, that image came roaring back to life as something of great importance.

Could that be what came next? If you could regain the upper hand and get life under control, somehow. Maybe the reason for figuring this all out was to go back to that point, to reconnect with and aim for a higher goal in life.

Fighting off the Warrior King's Army, just to settle down and raise a family and live happily ever after? Maybe... but only if you had never seen the fact that there was a summit up there. Maybe ignorance was bliss, but Max felt there was something higher and greater to shoot for beyond just dealing with a crisis and getting mid-life under control.

Max realized that what he wanted was more. His mind was focused on the obvious goals like making more money. But that was not really the point. Slogans started popping into his head like "Be all you can be" and "Just do it." But what he wanted was *meaning*. What he wanted was the freedom to focus on what felt really important.

But what he wanted was meaning. What he wanted was the freedom to focus on what felt really important.

Max suddenly found himself thinking about Bill Gates. Here was someone who had built an empire on a relatively dysfunctional product. But that was not the point. Bill Gates was not out to remain at the center of the business he had built. He was now free to go for his summit, to be one of the greatest philanthropists of all time. He was no longer worried about computer viruses that endlessly invaded his creation. He was now out to find cures to viruses that were killing tens of thousands of people every year.

"Some kind of poetic justice in that shift," Max thought out loud.

That's what was so irritating about the general stuff of life. It took up all the available time. So, great, you have managed to do what needs to be done in order to finish this day and start the cycle all over again the next day. There had to be more.

But what was up there on The Summit? Slaying The Dragon was the means to an end. Max had done that part and done it well, only to find himself bogged down, tangled in the vines, and stuck on the plateau.

> **He wanted to know that at the end of his life, he had gone as far and as high as he could travel in this life. This was about a personal kind of success beyond just the material symbols.**

Now, it was not just the coffee that was waking him up. That trivial little moment in the dream was waking something deep within him. He wanted more. He wanted to know that at the end of his life, he had gone as far and as high as he could travel in this life. This was about a *personal* kind of success beyond just the material symbols.

Until he figured out what that was in *his* life, Max realized that he was going to remain cranky and irritable. He also realized that the only way that he could ever begin to formulate what that larger dream looked like was by having the time and the space needed away from the endless running in circles.

***

Inching forward in traffic, Max plugged his iPhone into the jack in the car. He remembered the podcasts that his daughter had loaded for him the night before.

Maybe this wasn't really a mid-life crisis after all. What was the guy on the podcast calling it? "A mid-career crisis." Maybe he wasn't looking for a little red sports car to make him feel young again. He just wanted to get out of feeling trapped by his own career. He was waking up to a bigger picture and a summit that he had yet to reach.

> **He was waking up to a bigger picture and a summit that he had yet to reach.**

On the podcast, this psychologist was saying that this kind of crisis could be a good thing. He was talking about how the Chinese pictogram for "crisis" was made up of two elements: danger and opportunity.

Max was beginning to feel that maybe this *could* be a moment of opportunity for him – the opportunity to change his perspective, his mindset – so that he was no longer defining his business in terms that required him to trade his time for money. It was time to figure out how to reclaim the time that would allow him to do what really mattered on a different scale.

The other guy, the MBA on the podcast, was talking about marketing all the time. He was saying that Max needed to stop thinking of himself as a lawyer, a provider of legal services, and start thinking of himself as the "*marketer* of legal services and legal information."

Here on this podcast, this MBA and this psychologist were talking about what happens when service-providing professionals make a shift and find a strategy for capturing their lifetime of knowledge, skill, and experience. The goal was to take what was currently only being used to work with one client at a time, capture it, and convert it into a series of "information products."

An "infopreneur" was what the guy just called it. Max was intrigued by the sound of that. And he thought back to his conversation with Allison. She had said that people who had products to sell did not get bogged down in the same way that service providers did. He thought of her accountant colleague who had taken his knowledge of real estate investing and created a software product that could be sold to thousands and thousands of people.

These guys were talking about using his daughter's online networks just as he had been thinking about earlier. Creating *systems* that could channel his life experience out into the massive marketplace created by the Internet, thus freeing him from the limits of both time and geography.

Creating systems that could channel his life experience out into the massive marketplace created by the Internet, thus freeing the him from the limits of both time and geography.

Best of all, they were talking about doing this using *automated* systems so that his one-time effort in creating an information product was now being rewarded over and over and over again like the royalties on a hit song. Maybe he didn't need a good singing voice after all.

Best of all, they were talking about doing this using automated systems so that his one-time effort in creating an information product was now being rewarded over and over and over again like the royalties on a hit song.

This got his attention. Luckily, at the last second, the rapidly approaching bumper of the car in front of him got his attention, too! Max realized that he had never considered the possibility of doing something with his skills other than working with clients one-on-one. That's what he was trained to do. "You only see what you look for," echoed back in his mind. That's what the one guy on the podcast had just made a big point about. Maybe he needed to look at things a little differently.

These guys were talking about maps, guides, summits, and the 40/20/40 System.

They also kept hammering away at the idea that mastering the Online Jungle was only 20% of what he needed to focus on. Another 40% was about understanding how to Get Out of the crowd by understanding his unique narrative and creating his own legend. The last 40% was about making a series of shifts in the structure of his business: what it really was, how it needed to run, and how he could build value into it independent of trading his own time for money.

Success in business is 80% psychology and 20% mechanics.

"Success in business is 80% psychology and 20% mechanics," one of them said, and it took a shift in mindset to see that.

Max felt some of the tension in his chest ease. He still did not *have* a plan or a map, but he was starting to have hope that there was indeed a map to be had out there. And he decided to welcome this mid-career crisis and allow it to open his mind to the need for a change.

More of the same would clearly just give him *more of the same*. It made no sense at all to continue this way. What had the psychologist just said? "People assume that there is a good reason to explain why they do what they do. Sadly, that is rarely the case. We just do what we do because it's 'what we do.' Habit is one of the most powerful forces of nature."

There was no reason at all to continue doing what his role models had done, nor what everyone else was doing. He saw that they (and he) were just doing what they thought they "should" do as a lawyer. That was not feeling like such great logic to Max right then.

Max decided that it was time to take action. It was time to Get Out!

The moment Max made a decision to take action, he noticed something very interesting within himself. His level of frustration and anxiety immediately shifted. Instead of feeling angry and irritable, he was feeling excited. A little afraid, but kind of excited.

His energy had been given a path. It could flow forward again rather than leave him feeling all jammed up. Realizing that made him feel even more excited. He was only stuck on this plateau if his mind kept him prisoner there. The moment he accepted that change was an option, the walls came tumbling down. A bridge was forming across the moat he had dug by running circles around himself for so long.

He was only stuck on this plateau if his mind kept him prisoner there. The moment he accepted that change was an option, the walls came tumbling down. A bridge was forming across the moat he had dug by running circles around himself for so long.

The Jungle was still there all around him but now he was open to gathering up the tools and strategies that he would use to conquer and tame that jungle. Max now was focused on that moment in Maximillion's Tale when there was just a glimpse of something greater.

In his mind's eye, Max was able to lift his gaze up above the jungle's canopy and realize that taming the Online Jungle was only a necessary step toward a much bigger goal. Max was determined to master this jungle so that he could move past this and get back on track to a much greater summit.

Max wondered if it might just be possible that the best part of his career was only getting started.

Section III – The 40/20/40 System

Chapter 12 – Time For A Change

Where We've Been

Maximillion set out into The Unknown to slay The Dragon and along the way he acquired skills, talents, and specialized knowledge that he brought back to The Kingdom for the benefit of his people. Upon his return, he also saw a better way to run his business, even though it meant leaving behind the old ways of his father.

Max, our relatively successful, mid-career, mid-life professional, wakes up to find himself stuck on a plateau. Working in a business model that has him trading time for money, he discovers that there is no time left after selling off each week 60 to 80 hours of his life.

To make matters worse, Max finds himself entangled and bogged down by the Online Jungle. In what seems like an overnight revolution, he finds that his daughter has better skills than he does when it comes to creating networks and tapping into the power of online social media. Max is feeling trapped and frustrated.

Once upon a time, you were a Maximillion or Katherine. You were that young dreamer with a vision, however hazy it might have been at the start. You have done your time and earned the title of DragonSlayer.

Now, you find that you are more like Max or Kate. You are a mid-career professional with a growing list of dreams deferred. Perhaps you hope that someday, after you retire, *then* you will get back on the path to those dreams. Or perhaps, it is all just a dream.

What Went Wrong?

Like Maximillion, Max headed off on a quest – a quest to become a skilled and well-respected professional. Picture it this way: like Max, your goal is a distant summit and to reach that summit you must traverse a fairly dense forest. You know that as soon as you enter the forest you will lose sight of the summit because you will be beneath the canopy of the trees.

So you prepare yourself with a map.

Isn't that what we all did when we set off on the path of college, graduate school, professional training, or any of another set of paths that all offered a plan to achieve professional proficiency? We were investing in a map, a *curriculum*, that would guide us through that forest and on to the summit of our careers.

Confident, we set off on our quest. And it was hard, challenging work, but we had faith because along the way there were clearings where we could see through the canopy of the forest and catch a glimpse of that summit. We were moving closer, and that renewed our resolve to continue moving forward.

Toward the end of this journey things got pretty strenuous. The grade was getting steeper, surely a sign that we were moving up toward that summit. So we pushed harder up the incline. There were stops and starts along the way. There were mounting debts and major expenses, but we were committed to see this through.

Like Maximillion, you paid your dues. You slew your Dragon and were granted the authority of your profession, your area of expertise. You became a skilled professional!

You built your business, despite the fact that your training did not provide you with much help in terms of business-building skills. But building your business (your practice, your partnership) was the next part of the journey on to the summit of your career. The map of your training said that this was a kind of base-camp and that hard work here was the final stage in preparation for the climb to the top.

The thing is: in your professional training, it is unlikely that anyone spent even five minutes teaching you how to run a business. So, you look to your right and you look to your left, and you follow the herd of everyone else in your profession. You do what *they* do. And to get to the top, you do *more* of what they do for *more* hours than *they* do.

And so, you work long and hard, working to stand out from among your peers. 60 to 80 hour work weeks were just what was expected, and they were worth it because you were working toward a DreamDestination. And your income was growing steadily, providing even more evidence that you were on your way up.

But, in the end, you discover that you are less the owner of your business than its primary employee. (Ah, so *that's* what "self-employed" really means!) When you take your family on vacation, are you getting paid? Not if your business relies on billable hours for a service that you personally provide to your clients.

Without you, there is no business. There are just liabilities piling up each day creating negative cash flow. It makes it pretty hard to relax and ever feel like you are on vacation when in your heart you know that problems are growing by the hour back at the office.

Now, years have gone by with your working long, hard hours. But, are you running your business or is your business running *you* – running you around and around in circles so fast that there is no longer time to step back to survey your progress? Years have gone by.

We are betting that since you have read this far it has become quite clear to you that the map that brought you to this place was flawed. No one ever told you that if you *sell your time for a living*, it gets pretty tough to have time left for the *living of your life*.

Instead of heading for the summit, following the old map, you have arrived upon this plateau. The summit is right there within your sights, but you actually cannot get there from here. And now you have some other problems to face.

With all these years of running in circles around the center of your business, you have dug a moat around yourself, trapping you here at the center... trapping you upon this plateau. So now, you are going to have to build a bridge over that moat if you want to be freed from this trap.

Oh, but wait. There is another problem waiting for you after you build that bridge.

The Online Jungle

While you were so very busy building your business or developing your professional practice, working all these long hours to keep your clients, customers, or patients happy – well, the landscape around this plateau *really* changed.

The plateau upon which you are stranded has become surrounded by a dense, rapidly growing and changing jungle – The Online Jungle. How well equipped are you (once you bridge the moat to get yourself out of the middle of your business) to head off on the Jungle Expedition that will actually lead you on to The Summit of your career?

Some people are just beginning to wake up to the fact that it's a totally different landscape out there. If you keep running your business using the old paradigm, you *will* be overrun by those vines that have surrounded you and are threatening to crush the life out of your business.

More than ever, the world we live in is about networks, relationships, and interaction. The truth is that it has always been that way. But it used to function on a much smaller scale.

The Internet did not just shift things to a faster pace: it transformed everything fundamentally. Look at the music industry. Look at newspapers. Look at mail delivery. Cling to an outdated model and, well, let's just say that Darwinian evolution is not sentimental.

Now it's survival of the most-networked.

Your customers and clients are no longer interested in being marketed to and sold to in the old way. You now need to figure out how to reach out to have an interactive conversation with them. You need to figure out how to build relationships with people whom you have yet to meet.

And high-tech solutions alone cannot get you there. It is time to learn how to use *high tech* to deliver *high touch*.

They, your future clients, customers, or patients, will only ask for your services when they feel that they know you, like you, trust you, *and* that you have already *proven* to them that you have a solution to their problem. And frankly, who can blame them? Isn't that the same thing you want when you look for a product or service?

The good news is that the very same Internet has made it easier than ever before in human history to do just that. It really has always been about networks, relationships, and interaction. But the old media simply lacked the tools to do that very effectively. So we all learned to put up with the dominant kind of marketing that was possible before the Internet: a one-way fire-hose spewing information all over you.

Companies dumped on everyone, hoping that even though they were annoying a lot of people, they were likely reaching their actual customers along the way.

Now, technology allows for interactive communication on a grand scale while still targeting the messages down into very narrowly-defined niches. And because you *can* do that, your customers and clients *demand* that you do just that. You need to become a welcomed visitor rather than an annoying pest. Get your message directly to the right people without annoying everyone else. The fact is, it just works better anyway.

Can Pain Be A Good Thing?

We share your pain. We started out with the very same map and arrived at very similar plateaus of our own along the way. In fact, these paths are all around you... paths that lead to false summits. Perhaps you have already ventured into the jungle and cleared a path only to find your way onto yet another plateau. Frustrating, we know.

While no one enjoys it, sometimes pain is a good thing. Sometimes that pain is a signal telling you that something is wrong with the way things are – something in your life requires your urgent attention. That kind of pain is trying to wake you up so that you don't keep doing things the same old way. Remember that old definition of insanity? "Insanity is doing the same thing over and over again while expecting a different result." Clearly, change is needed.

If you recognize the kind of pain we are talking about, then you should realize that the worst thing you can do is focus on making that pain stop before you really understand what needs to change. For example, if you have broken a leg, you don't want to take enough pain killer to allow you to keep walking on that leg. It is time for something different. It is time to make a change and fix things.

Consider this: the pain that we are talking about is what doctors refer to as the *chief complaint*. It is the symptom which relates to a deeper, underlying problem. What we will explore with you in the remainder of this book is how to go deep to cure the underlying problem. We are not interested in just the quick fix that only treats the symptom: you need more than that.

This mid-career, mid-life crisis is really nothing but good news. Really! The only thing that makes it painful is when you try to hold on to an outdated, unwanted business model. You and your clients stand to benefit tremendously by giving up on what "happily ever after" used to mean while you fully embrace *your* journey and *your* story.

Where We Are Going

While there is something tempting about jumping right on the task of mastering the specific *tools* that will enable you to hack through the tangle and become Master of The Online Jungle, we are not going to begin there. That is the 20 in the 40/20/40 System… and it doesn't come first.

Think of it this way: a really great machete won't help you very much if you do not have the map that will lead you through the jungle. You first need to develop a very clear idea of the destination. If you don't begin with the end in mind, you will find yourself lost, even if you have great skill in clearing the path right in front of you.

We are going to work with you from the inside out. Change has to begin with *you* first. Then we'll work on the vision of what your business is all about – what needs to change about its structure and organization. By doing that, you will develop a clear vision of not only the path through the jungle, but also the path to your real destination. Only then are you ready to pick up some really sharp tools and charge into the thick of this jungle.

You are part of a large group of professionals and highly skilled, technical people who probably have no right to complain. In truth, you are better off than most people are. And yet, you know exactly how you *feel* right now, right? Tired, trapped, frustrated, and lost. How's that for a summary?

PersonalSuccess Marketing will lay out a path for you to follow as you make a series of very important shifts and transformations in mindset, in the model of your business, and in your approach to marketing.

The best *is* yet to come. And it involves working less to earn more. Does that get your interest?

We cheered on Maximillion and felt we were right there when he slew the dragon. And we've suffered with Max, feeling his pain as he struggled on the TimeTrap Plateau with the overgrown Online Jungle surrounding it. Now it's time to look ahead and focus on YOU.

Take a deep breath, feel the cleansing of the air rushing into your lungs, know that there really IS a way out of the Jungle when you have the right maps to lead you and tools to keep you moving.

So now what? How do you "Get Out of the Online Jungle" alive and doing well and head for your Summit – that place where your life is good, your business runs without your being surrounded by the moat, and you have enough time to enjoy your family, without the fear of economic pressures. That's what PersonalSuccess Marketing is all about!

First comes psychological change. You must Get Out... from the center of your business and from your identification with your profession. You must Create Your Own Legend. That is how you build the bridge over the moat and free yourself from the TimeTrap Plateau. That takes you to the edge of the plateau where now you must face the Online Jungle. The Universe Model we will show you will guide you through.

Once you master the Online Jungle, you are free to begin exploring the path that leads out from the jungle and on to the summit of your career. Once you make The Shift you buy back your time... and it is all about time.

The Value Of Time

Let's pause here for a moment to discuss time, because time is at the heart of the matter. That was part of the flaw in the map that brought you to this plateau in the first place. We were all taught to focus on the *money*, and because of that we lost awareness of the real value of *time*.

After all, what is money?

We would argue that money is a symbolic representation of the value of time. You pay someone to paint your home, and the amount you pay is the value you place upon the time you will *not* spend doing the job plus the time it took for the painter to develop the level of skill and proficiency that she or he possesses.

Our focus needs to shift away from dollars and remain on time. Time is much more precious because it cannot be replaced and it cannot be made up for later. When it's gone, it's gone.

Which brings us to the heart of the flaw in your original map, and to the starting point for building the bridge over the moat. The map that led you here has you stuck because you currently trade time for money. Granted, as your level of skill and expertise has increased, so has the fee that you are able to receive in exchange for your time.

But here you are at mid-career. Have you noticed that there is an upper limit to what that fee can be? At some point the market turns to another provider of your service at a lower cost. Now, you end up either hitting a ceiling or selling off a few more hours of your life to hold on to your income.

Have you also noticed how your overhead has increased right along with your increases in income? You wake up one day and realize that you are selling off all your best hours and you have pretty well jumped aboard an endless cycle. Because you have accumulated not only the overhead of your business, but also the overhead of your life (your family, the house, the car, the tuition, etc.), you can't afford to slow down your pace without feeling the heat.

That is what we mean by "stuck on the TimeTrap Plateau."

40/20/40 Equals 100 Percent Transformation

You need to understand fully that the focus has to be on *owning* your time. You need to take back a portion of that time even if it means enduring some of that heat in the short run. You are going to need that portion of time to build your bridge and join us at the Jungle's edge. The truth is that reclaiming this initial portion of time IS the bridge. Building this bridge is the first 40 of the 40/20/40 System.

We are going to devote 40 percent of our efforts to the task of building the bridge that leads over the moat because this will require that you change your mind. You are going to need to Get Out.

There are two parts to what we mean by Get Out. **First**, accept the fact that you must get out of being the hub of the wheel of your business. If you *are* your business, then there is no effective way to Get Out. Even if you don't yet know *how* to Get Out, accept the reality that you MUST Get Out! **Second**, you must Get Out of the crowd you are in. Get Out of doing what you do in the same way everyone else within your profession does it. Get Out requires a change in your professional identity.

We will show you how to develop your unique PersonalSuccess Brand. We call this Create Your Own Legend. This is the compelling narrative that functions as an organizing force in your business and in the marketing of your business.

In order to Get Out, you need to step out from your need to be the center of your business. You need to move the center of your personal identity out from being essentially the same as your professional identity. Dr. Marc no longer *identifies* himself as a psychologist and Charlie no longer *is* a photographer (though he really does still appear to be a marketing-crazed MBA!). We had to break free from *being* what we do. In fact, because of that new mindset, we are now the owners of several businesses and have each had several careers along the way. It now takes at least a conversation over coffee for us to answer that old question, "So, what is it you do?"

Once we help you to Get Out, we are going to give you the strategic plan that gets you through the Online Jungle. There are the tools and also the strategy and the tactical plan for the use of those tools. Together, this is about 20 percent of the focus, it is the 20 in the 40/20/40 System.

We will introduce you to the Universe Model of Social Media Marketing which will show you how to organize your online tools into a coherent *system* where you can harness the flow of information and direct it to serve the marketing plan for your business. We will open the jungle's canopy to give you a clear view of the stars and planets that help you navigate and help you drive energy into the sun that lies at the heart of your marketing system.

What may seem right now to be a chaotic group of social media components will be pulled together for you into a coherent system. We will show you how energy flows within this system in a logical and systematic way. Master this and you will join an elite one percent of the business world that is truly able to tap the power of social media marketing.

The final 40 involves making a critical shift in your business. You need to package properly all the knowledge, skill, and expertise you have acquired while you were working hard to become a DragonSlayer and establishing yourself as an expert professional. We will focus on the shifts that can take you out of the trading-time-for-money trap and allow you to create new streams of income in your business.

You will then be able to build passive-income streams which pay you independent of your time, streams that can be layered one atop the next to exponentially increase your income and pay you while you are investing your time in other activities.

The final 40 percent of the 40/20/40 System shows you how to capture and package the years of skill, training, and experience you have acquired. You will then be able to deliver it efficiently and effectively on the online platform that we will help you build.

Do these three things well and you will no longer be trapped on the plateau of trading time for money. You will no longer be trapped at the center of your business. You will no longer be tangled in the

Online Jungle. And your business can then grow intrinsic value – value that is independent of your personal presence.

Do these three things well and you will be free to define your DreamDestination with the clear vision that awaits you at the Summit of your career. Do the first part well and anything is possible. Do the second part well and we will crown you Master of the Online Jungle. Do the third part well and we will crown you SummitMaster.

How Hard Is Change?

At PersonalSuccess Marketing, we start at the tree-top level where our vision is better and clearer. We first need to understand where we ARE and then decide exactly where we want to GO.

Let's face it… on the floor of the Jungle, visibility isn't very good. The vines of uncertainty surround you and you have no idea how to cut a clear path. And since you see what you look for, and you get used to looking for very little, you end up lost.

To accomplish this, we need to talk about change. Now, you may think that change is hard. But here is the truth: Nature has laws. Nature's penalties are harsh if you break her laws. One important law can be stated quite simply as "adapt or perish." So the only thing harder than change is *refusing* to change and thereby becoming extinct. Now, doesn't change look so much more positive? (We thought so.)

Since you have looked at Yesterday (Maximillion's Tale) and Today (Max's Dilemma), let's focus on moving forward, changing your mindset, creating true value in your business. Let's start with YOU – who you are, how you think, and where you are headed. Then we get to the strategy to help you Get Out of The Jungle and then head to your DreamDestination.

Chapter 13 – Don't Stand Out – Get Out!
The First 40

Professional (Technician) to Entrepreneur

If you are like so many other professionals, you are *great* at what you do in your specialty – let's call that being the "technician" – but have had little or no training in running a business. You watched a parent or a friend, you were taught that to earn more you had to *work* more. And soon you saw that you have only so many hours and there is only so much business that you can book *in* those hours because you have to trade hours for dollars.

Even someone getting $1,000 an hour has a ceiling for the amount that can be earned in a year. OK… many of us would *jump* at the chance to trade hours for $1,000 an hour – but how likely is that in what you are doing?

There is a change of mindset needed here if you are to grow.

Here is an example from Charlie: Years ago, I was talking with one of my photography marketing gurus (one of the hats I have worn is as a professional photographer for Family Portraits, Weddings, and Bat and Bar Mitzvahs). Here's what he said to me: "Charlie, you are NOT a photographer." I thought, "Hey... my photography is not *that* bad!!"

He went on: "You are a marketer and seller of photographic services. And when you can make that leap in your mind, you will be on the road to success."

That was all I needed.

Quickly I learned that I could make more money doing **marketing** for my business than I could make with a camera in my hands. And let's face it: there will always be a better technician somewhere – a better photographer, psychologist, dentist, therapist, coach. But when that technician thinks like an entrepreneur and not a technician, when that technician uses the great marketing techniques that we teach in PersonalSuccess Marketing, when that technician identifies with being an entrepreneur, then… THEN a business can be built.

Here is an example from Dr. Marc: The truth is, like many professionals, I *never* really learned to make this change of mindset in my psychology practice when I first came out of graduate school. I was there to help my patients. There was a real reluctance to focusing on the *business* of the practice. It almost felt that to do so was to tarnish the greater value, the higher calling of the work I was doing.

The only problem with that is that I was behaving like a non-profit – only without any fund raising or rich patrons! Let's just be clear that this is not a sustainable business model.

What it really took for me to change my approach was creating a different business. When I founded and developed my real estate investing company, I suddenly felt freed of all the "cultural" baggage that went with being a psychologist. It was like a breath of fresh air because I previously looked at "business" as a necessary evil to keep my practice moving. Now I was free to play what I called "Monopoly for Grown-Ups."

And "play" is the right word. Once I was free to see business as something fun, a game that you play to win, I was able to bring that perspective back into my psychology practice. Then I could see clearly that being an entrepreneur in your profession tarnishes nothing. It is exactly the opposite. You start focusing on delivering a much higher-quality service or product. This change is critical and fundamental to your success.

Mindset

Don't Stand Out – Get Out is the change that must come from within. The focus is mental. It is subtle but absolutely critical.

If we take Max as an example, here is how this might look: Max would typically define himself as an attorney since he provides legal services for an hourly fee.

The problem with Max making his profession equal to a huge portion of his personal identity is that he has psychologically trapped himself at the center of his business. Often, we professionals don't even think in terms of business because we *are* what we do. So as the frustrations grow, as the feeling of being trapped intensifies, it is confusing because Max cannot *see* the true source of his problem. It is a problem of identity at its core, and it is always difficult to see a pattern when you are embedded within it.

Get Out is about stepping out of that identity to see the business of your profession from the outside. Max can begin by understanding that rather than *being* an attorney, he can see himself as the *provider* of legal services. And to Get Out fully, he needs to focus on being the *marketer* of legal services and legal information. But we will get back to that in more detail shortly.

This internal change of perspective is in many ways the hardest. Mindset is tricky. As professionals, we easily become trapped by the "culture" of our professions. We are trained to think a certain way. What makes change at this level so difficult is that we generally don't "see" our culture clearly because we are so deeply embedded within it.

Have you ever traveled abroad for any length of time? It is when you return that you suddenly have heightened awareness of the way you live, all the little things that we take for granted. The "rules" and assumptions are implicit. We feel that this is just how things are and how they are done.

There are two very important words that PersonalSuccess Marketing asks you to focus on and pay attention to. We refer to this as the power of **Shoulds+Oughts**™. These are two sneaky little words. And we ask that you turn these two words into a kind of mental alarm bell.

Your mission, "should" you choose to accept it, is to catch yourself every time one of these two rascals sneaks into a thought or a sentence. These are the two little words that will keep you trapped in a mindset that no longer helps you adapt.

Here is the thing. There are no Shoulds+Oughts at birth. Everything that your mind links and associates around these words is *learned*. But not just any kind of learning. It has been taught to you from outside of yourself. These *never* come from direct, personal experience, and that is why they are potentially dangerous to your professional health.

You would never think to yourself, "I *shouldn't* put my hand on that hot stove." You don't need to because you *know* this at a level of truth that comes from direct, personal experience.

Shoulds+Oughts are different. These need to be approached with a healthy dose of skepticism. They might be true. But then again, they might not. Someone has conditioned you to adopt a mindset tied to these two words.

And, quite often, that's great. One of the powerful things about the human mind is that we CAN learn from other people's experiences without having to rediscover everything by personal trial and error.

The danger is – how do you know what is *truth* and what is a commonly held, but untrue, *belief*?

Our professions contain a mix of truth along with a dose of other Shoulds+Oughts that are more like a smudge of ink that keeps getting faithfully reproduced from one photocopy to the next. It's just there. You are used to it. You expect it to be there. In fact, it *ought* to be there. No, really, it *should* be there. Why? Because it is what we learned to expect.

Marketing for professionals, and especially online marketing, is just full of these ink-smudge Shoulds+Oughts. It is foreign territory and the universal response to the unknown is FEAR. Fear makes people behave conservatively. We retreat to what we know. Better safe than sorry. Better stick to how I Should+Ought to market, based on what I learned before the Internet even existed.

Huh? Is that logic, or is it *fear*?

The alternative to fear is curiosity. Curiosity leads to exploration, and through careful exploration, the unknown becomes part of the new and improved known.

The question really boils down to this: like Max, are you frustrated enough that you are willing to do something new? The Online Jungle is here to stay. Those teens and tweens Twittering and Tweeting away all around you: they are your new customers, clients, and patients. The Online Jungle, like a real jungle, is a living, breathing thing that grows around you and will swallow you up if you don't adapt. Change is not optional, but extinction is. So, we highly recommend adapting!

So let's look at some important changes that you will feel free to explore once you finish clearing out those nasty Shoulds+Oughts.

Don't Stand Out – Get Out!

Okay, so Max steps out of the center enough to see his business from the outside. But even if he has come to see himself as the marketer of legal services and information, he is still being seen by other people against the background of every other attorney.

How is Max… how are *you...* going to stand out?

We say *don't*. Jumping up and down to get notice is so undignified! Don't try to stand out from the crowd – Get Out from that crowd and claim your own unique space. Why be slightly different in price, size, color, or the advice you give? Be the original person you were born to be and let your individual light shine.

Too many people feel that they have nothing unique to say, no story to tell, no experiences to share. And that could not be further from reality once you learn how easy it is to express what is unique about you. PersonalSuccess Marketing, as you might have noticed from the first two sections of this book, uses narrative structures (story telling) as a way of organizing marketing messages.

A great example of how *not* to achieve this is found in the real estate section in your local Sunday newspaper. Hold it at arms length, squint a little bit so everything goes slightly out-of-focus, and then see what ads jump out at you.

None of them! They're all the same. In fact, some of the best photography is reserved for the *broker* and not the real estate itself.

What does this mean to you? It means that you can't hope to be *the* person chosen in your field if you look, sound, and act just like everyone else.

We believe that this is a problem that plagues professionals more than anyone – and we speak from personal experience. When you are a part of a well-defined profession, you live inside the bubble of a certain culture. Whether you are a psychologist, a physician, an attorney, a therapist, or a candlestick maker… there are just certain expected ways of doing things – Shoulds+Oughts. Some of these are actual rules written into codes of conduct and ethics. Others are just traditions.

But here is what we have noticed time and again: many people take these rules and cultural norms and project them far beyond where they are appropriate or necessary. And over time, as you are trained by people within your profession, as you work side by side with people in your own profession, as you take on traits of those around you… well, you get the picture. We all start to look exactly the same to the world outside of the bubble.

If what you offer is unique, your competition is gone. The price points defined within the old bubble, they are gone. You are now free to show your prospective client or customer the actual value of what you have to offer them.

So just how do you go about Getting Out?

Create Your Own Legend

There is a very good reason that we focus on mid-career, mid-life professionals. You actually *have* a story to tell, and you have been doing what you do for many years. You have *lived* experience. You bring a unique personality to the professional work you do. With those two ingredients, your unique personality and your professional history, we can craft a story.

Remember in Maximillion's Tale, the little man dressed in green and brown playing the pipe? He asked Maximillion and Katherine to come back to finish the story (their song). He knew that they would soon create their own legend. That is PersonalSuccess Marketing.

We study how people become known, why certain professionals appear to be at the *top of mind*, and why celebrities and performers get well known.

And all of us can borrow from what they do.

While your business must be different, YOU have to be different as well. Who are you? Why did you become the professional that you are? What makes you "tick" and why will others like to learn about you?

Many people struggle with this one, but we are going to show you exactly how it's done... to help you *tell* others and *show* others who you are.

And in addition to what we can cover here in this book, on our website and in our training materials we will show you how to:

- Show What Is Unique About You
- Take BIG Actions
- Go For Excellence

- Use Speed
- Create Your Image
- Lead The Way

And let's face it – people LOVE stories. Through the centuries our histories have been passed down through stories. You see a friend over the weekend and you tell stories about what has been happening with you. And in your house of worship, you probably hear LOTS of stories (like Psalms, Proverbs, and more).

Your story needs to be told and we'll show you how to do it. You see, this is a natural outgrowth of stepping out of the crowd and claiming your own unique niche. You are now freed from the label of your profession. That label tells a story about a group. In that story, your uniqueness is lost. If that is your only story, then you are just one among many. You have become a commodity. It all comes down to supply and demand. If you are one among many, there is just too much supply. When you are unique, you command a unique value.

You have your specific story to tell. And the narrative structure you create in telling that story serves to make you much more memorable, and it becomes a guiding structure to the process of marketing your business.

PersonalSuccess Branding

Most people think of "branding" as the logo on stationery, the layout of a website, and the folders in which proposals are presented.

And they would be right. But only partially right.

Branding is very much about the story we were just talking about. By creating your own legend and getting out of the crowd, you claim your unique personality. *That* is PersonalSuccess Branding.

Branding, at its core, is about showing who you are and what you are about. Branding is being the best professional *you* can be. And it goes beyond you and your narrative. It extends throughout your business. Actions really do speak louder than words. And when words and actions fall out of sync, your brand becomes badly damaged.

Your story and your business actions have to be one coherent whole. Attention to all these details is a very important part of your brand. When you go out to a really nice restaurant, it's most certainly about the food. But it is also about the atmosphere, the china and linens, the attention of the wait staff, the presentation on the plate. All the little details become a critical part of the story you tell.

And you have to know yourself well and know which details to focus on if you are to succeed at delivering a clear picture to your clients, customers, or patients. So between Psychologist Marc and Marketing MBA Charlie, we'll help you find your InnerCore to share, and then we'll show you how to communicate it effectively.

On our website and in our success materials and events, you will find a wealth of information about these key details. Among the additional topics are:

- Getting People Interested in You and Your Product/Service
- Why People Buy
- Persuasion
- Marketing the PersonalSuccess Marketing Way
- Using Video To Explode Your Marketing Success
- Customer Service and Avoiding Sales Prevention
- How To Get Them To Buy
- Selling The Professional
- Referrals and Follow Up Systems
- Creating Your Business Systems

- Building Your Team Through Outsourcing and Joint Ventures
- Building Your Business To Sell (And Keep Earning)

All this and more as PersonalSuccessMarketing.com continues to expand and develop. Make sure you have registered on our site so that you receive the latest content updates.

Chapter 14 – The Universe Model – The 20

We invite you for a moment to think back and reflect upon Max's Dilemma. Early on, with his frustrations deepening, he had an insight about what could happen if his level of experience, knowledge, and expertise could somehow be merged with his 13-year-old daughter's skill and ease in the use of social media and online networking. His wife, Kate, also has the realization that the online world has changed from one generation to the next as she works to reestablish good communication with their son who is off at college.

This is what we must all learn to do now if we are going to master the Online Jungle. Without these skills, you will not only remain stuck on a plateau, you will also find yourself unable to connect effectively to and communicate with the up-and-coming generations. These are your new clients and customers. These are your new patients. So don your khaki explorer's jacket and let's prepare to head into The Jungle.

You must move through The Jungle and master the Universe Model of Social Media Marketing if you wish to be Master of the Online Jungle. The Jungle is full of viruses, snakes, and tangled vines.

Armed with the right tools, a map, and a real strategic plan, that Jungle can be tamed, harnessed, and put to work to become your marketing tropical paradise.

But don't get too comfortable with that image and start thinking about fruited drinks. We are not staying here. This is not our destination. We are going to harness this gold mine of natural resources and put it to work in the service of achieving much greater goals. Recall that Max's level of interest and excitement was not related simply to learning to market his legal practice online. This Jungle leads to a set of transformations that will forever free Max from the TimeTrap Plateau.

When we say that the Online Jungle is rich in resources, we are not kidding. The Internet has matured so rapidly over the past several years that many people have yet to understand the power that lies at their fingertips. They watch children and grandchildren texting, twittering, and building social networks in a way that makes it look like play time. But this is not child's play. This is the transformation of your marketing and the structure of your business.

The Universe Model Of Social Media Marketing

You're deep in the Online Jungle and you see light ahead of you, giving you hope about the direction you will take to get out, but you're surrounded by hundreds of Internet tools. News articles are full of them, and you've even seen some of them in commercials on television. Even your friends are talking about them, and your kids are **using** them.

Some of these tools you've heard about like Facebook, Twitter, YouTube, LinkedIn, and blogs; others are just words: Digg, Flickr, and StumbleUpon, though perhaps you have a feeling that you've been "stumbling" since you first heard all this mumbo jumbo.

You may even have tried some of these, but are they doing you any good? How can you tell? What should your results be and how much time should you spend working with them?

How do you keep yourself from drowning?

To move through the Online Jungle and become a master of the Online Jungle, you really need to follow a system, use a map to navigate, and know where you're going **before** you set off in the direction you have set for yourself.

But how?

What do you do? How do you avoid running in circles, digging a moat around yourself, and winding up back where you were: confused but having wasted countless hours?

Human beings throughout history have turned to the stars for navigation. We have punched a hole through The Jungle's canopy to give you a view of the sky above you.

Here, in brief, is what we call the **Universe Model of Social Media Marketing**. It's a system, a way to think about all these tools, a map to get you out of the Online Jungle. Clearly we can't cover all of it here, but the *thought* behind our Universe Model will be clear to you.

Think about it this way: The Sun, The Planets, The Stars

The Sun

Just as the Sun is the center of our earthly orbit, so is the Sun the center of our Model. Planets revolve around the Sun. Beyond the Planets are the Stars.

At the center of your online universe is your Main Website – let's call it your Money Site. From there you will host all of your content and sell whatever products you make available.

Everything must revolve around your Money Site. It is the center, the heart, the most important part of your system. Everything you do must point to your Sun (your Money Site).

Your Money Site must be dynamic: that is to say that it must constantly be changing. Google and all the other search engines love websites that change. The old-fashion, static websites of the 1990s do not work in today's marketing. Put up a website that doesn't change and don't expect to have much traffic.

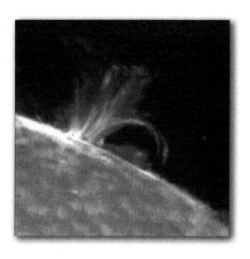

One of the easiest ways to create a dynamic website is to build it on WordPress. You may have heard about WordPress and think of it as a blogging platform, but it is *much* more than that: it is a content-management system that Google loves. Build it on WordPress and they will come! Keep adding new content and they will come over and over again!

The Planets

Away from the Sun, and adding attention to it, are the Planets. They revolve around the Sun and because they are related to each other, they give and take energy.

Other Social Media websites are the Planets. They are independent websites, but you want them to point to you; point to you as in have **links** on them that when clicked, people are taken directly to your Money Site. Links are like votes for you, testimonials from the websites that have those links pointing to you, and we all want testimonials that say we are good!

These are such Social Media Websites as YouTube and other video-hosting websites, Blogger and other blogging websites, Facebook Profiles and Pages, iTunes and other podcast distribution sites, and Hubpages, a special article website that Google seems to love. There are many, many planets in this Universe beyond those listed here!

Generally you can post your own content on these websites and link them directly to your Money Site. For example, you can post a video on YouTube and put your Money Site's URL in the description. When people watch one of your videos, they can click on your link to get more information directly from your Money Site.

There is another benefit of doing this: every time Google finds a link pointing to your Money Site, it follows that link when it indexes the Internet for relevant content. The more links you have pointing to *you*, the more important Google feels you are. And when these links come from popular websites like YouTube, it counts even more.

The Stars

From the Planets, we can see the Stars. They are always in the sky and can be seen from each of the Planets.

In our Model, the Stars are those special websites that can point to your Planets AND to your Sun and draw attention for you.

Twitter and Bookmarking sites come to mind immediately. You don't put much content on these websites, but you use them like billboards pointing to what you do on your Planets and on your Sun.

They basically say, "Hey, look over there: there is some great content for you to see!"

They twinkle, they shine their special light on you, but there isn't much substance to their content. Since people SEE them, you want to be sure to list your best work with them and point directly to one of your Planets (and through the Planet to the Sun) or directly to your Sun.

Think In Straight Lines, Not Circles

Be sure that when you link, you think in straight lines and not circles.

Link from a Star to a Planet to the Sun but then do NOT link back the other direction.

For instance: Link from Twitter to one of your YouTube videos and from that video to your Money Site, but then do NOT link back to your video from your Money Site.

If you think of this as energy, you want to be sure to have all of the energy aimed at the Sun to build its power and make it shine the brightest.

You can link from Planet to Planet, but then don't link back the other way. So from your Facebook Page you can link to a YouTube video, which then links directly to your Money Site, but don't link back to Facebook from there.

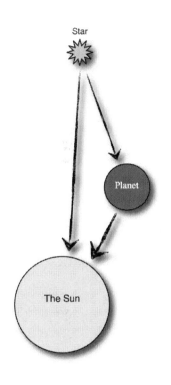

Here's an over simplified reason why you don't link in circles: Google wants to find the important websites. If *you* are the center of the universe, as indicated by all the links pointing to you, then Google feels you are important. However, if every link points BACK to where the first link came from, Google thinks, "Hmm, there must be a lot of link-swapping going on here: these folks aren't really all that important." And let's face it, you DO want to be important!

Rules Of The Road

Here are a few quick tips:

1. **Keep your Money Site dynamic by adding articles, videos, and MP3 audios.** Do this at least weekly so that when Google comes back to search your site, it says "Wow, new content: we had better tell everyone about this website." If you do ***not*** have new information, Google says, "Let's skip this website for a while and revisit later to see if it has changed." Dynamic content wins over static content every time. Dynamic content even wins over "authority" content – so if **you** keep adding content, you can outrank an expert who only adds information infrequently. And let's face it: most of your competition will ***not*** keep adding to their websites, so you will win when you do!

2. **Mix your Media.** Google, and those visiting your website, love to find different types of content: video, audio, written posts. Video is huge on the Internet, and that is one of the reasons that PersonalSuccessMarketing.com uses it so much. It might also explain why Google actually bought YouTube. Video is neither very hard nor expensive to create, and MP3 audio content can be very mobile: your visitors can take it with them for listening on their iPods or other MP3 players and in their cars.

3. **Keep your content in bite-sized pieces.** We're all busy. We want our information and even our entertainment in small packages. We don't have time to consume lengthy documents, videos, or podcasts. So keep things simple and in small, bite-sized pieces and the chances someone will view, read, or listen will improve. A typical blog post is between 250 to 500 words. A typical audio podcast is 20 to 60 minutes per episode, and video needs to stay under 10 minutes, but two or three minutes is probably ideal.

4. **Make your content valuable!** The more valuable you make your content, the more people will like it. The more people like it, the more they will tell their online friends, and they will tell *their* friends, and all of this will drive traffic to your Money Site.

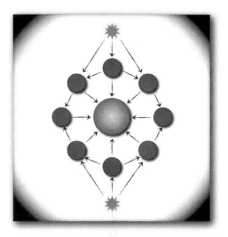

Why Social Marketing?

There is a moment in our story about Max where he is contemplating the online tools that he and his firm have attempted to work with. He thinks about his LinkedIn profile and Facebook page. And he thinks about the money they have paid to consultants for these as well as their main website. And what he realizes is that they are not *working*. They are each more like random asteroids floating through space than they are a *system* of stars and planets that feed energy to your sun. It's not that each piece does not function – it is that they are not integrated, they don't talk to each other, and they don't engage prospects in a relationship-building fashion.

Marketing is relationship building. Max realizes that he can meet people at a networking event and hand them his business card. They can exchange contact information and chat a little bit about how they might be able to do business together. They can agree to follow up with each other at a later date. However, Max can only be in one physical location at a time. How many meet-and-greet meetings can he attend in any given month?

The question becomes, how can Max use technology to leverage both his time and his geographic presence? The answer to this part of Max's Dilemma, as you might well guess, is social media marketing. An integrated, online-marketing system allows Max to be everywhere at once. It systematically captures contact information just as though Max and a new visitor were exchanging business cards. And it sets in motion a series of follow-up contacts, creating a virtual conversation between Max and his ever-growing network.

Today, places like Facebook and LinkedIn build on our need to be connected. Some say connecting is part of our DNA. The high levels of activity on social media sites also help build your visibility to Google and other search engines, thus driving more people to your Money Site. You need to meet people where THEY are so they can know, like, trust, buy, buy again, and refer you... but first people have to know you exist.

Think about this: if you are going to be successful, you need to date your prospects, marry your clients, and build families with those who hire you over and over again, or purchase multiple products from you. Letting them Know, Like, and Trust You is best accomplished through solid social networking – both the type of networking you grew up with and now the type online.

When we define our entire program in materials devoted just to this topic, you'll see which Social Media websites you really need and which you can skip. There are way too many to use and we show you which ones are key to your success. But now that you understand the Universe Model of Social Media Marketing "system," you'll be able to make Social Media Marketing work for YOU.

How Can I Ever Find The Time To Do All This?

Right now, you might think to yourself that if you are already working 60 to 80 hours a week, how are you ever going to find the time to go dancing through this Universe! Never fear. That is part of why this is a *system*. It is also why in the next chapter we are going to focus on freeing up your time. You are NOT going to be working 60 to 80 hours any longer, and you don't have to do all of these things personally!

Once you really understand that the Universe Model has a logical flow of energy to it, you start to understand the sequences. Sequences can be automated. In the coming sections, you will see that this system can run incredibly smoothly for you if you capture, package, distribute, syndicate, and outsource.

At PersonalSuccess Marketing, we help you define your individual workflow sequence. Your task is to put in place simple, basic information-capture systems right in the sequence of your current, daily work life.

We will show you how to package the information you have quickly and efficiently into products that others want. These enhance your marketing and become profit centers that increase your cash flow, create income that is independent of your hourly efforts, and build intrinsic value into your business. We will also show you how to save more time by outsourcing parts of each process.

Follow the system and you will no longer work 60 to 80 hours a week. We want you to free up time to buy back your life!

Once this information is packaged properly, we will show you step-by-step how to place these products into the automated system that drives online traffic through *your* Universe and draws it to your Money Site, moving your products out to your customers and clients.

We will not tell you that all this can magically happen without any effort. What we will show you, however, is that most of these operations can be automated through a combination of technology and careful outsourcing. You can have it done for you and earn money, independent of your personal time.

Chapter 15 – Making The Shift – The Final 40

After the meeting with his accountant, Allison, Max came away frustrated, but seeking better solutions for his dilemma. Max's daughter searched online to find a marketing-crazed MBA and a psychologist who just happened to have a bunch of podcasts for her father to listen to. What an amazing coincidence! In listening to these two whacky guys, and nearly crashing his car in the process, Max was introduced to the concept of being an infopreneur.

The day prior, Max and Allison were discussing the Achille's heel in the business model they are both in, "the path of service" as she called it. You trade hours for dollars in a linear fashion. Allison told Max about her colleague, an accountant who developed a software program that made the lives of real estate investors much easier. His skill and expertise were converted into an information product, and that digital product could now be marketed and sold by a relatively automated online system.

Information products start getting Max pretty excited. He can begin converting the skill, knowledge, and experience that he already possesses and convert it into a form that breaks the linear link between the information and his time. Once created, information can be sold and downloaded instantly over and over and over again. A one-time investment of time now creates an income stream trading information for dollars.

Max is right to get excited: he just discovered how to remove the ceiling on his income growth potential. And now, in the sections that follow, we'll give you a glimpse of The Shift needed to get you from where you are trading time for money to being an Infopreneur by using automated systems to produce income independent of your time. Each part of this already exists and we'll show you how to get it all to work smoothly and automatically for you.

First find out what we're describing and then look forward to how easy it will be to get it done for you.

The Shift – Part I: Entrepreneur to Infopreneur

Back when we introduced you to the Universe Model of Social Media Marketing, there may have come a moment where you asked yourself, "Just exactly *where* is all this 'content' we keep talking about supposed to come from?" The Shift is the answer to that question.

Have you ever heard of Information Products? What they are is simple: anything that can teach someone with words, images, and sounds can be an information product.

Books, ebooks, CDs, DVDs, courses with success manuals, webinars, teleseminars, online courses, websites, podcasts – they are ALL considered information products. What you are reading now is an information product!

And it's the entrepreneur who figures out how to convert the expertise in his or her head, from years of service and study, into an information product for sale. This is the professional who has successfully made the shift from being an entrepreneur to an Infopreneur.

Before we move forward, however, let's pause for a moment to reflect upon why we are making this change. This shift is the key transformation in the entire 40/20/40 system. It is the change in what you are actually *doing*. Making this shift is what finally sets you free from the TimeTrap Plateau.

Let's go back to Max to see how this shift solves his dilemma. He found himself stranded on the TimeTrap Plateau, surrounded by a moat holding him in the middle of his business, and that plateau was surrounded by the Online Jungle. Off in the distance, Max could see The Summit. But that was out of reach because the map he followed to the middle of his career was flawed. It led him right to his plateau. Stuck with a great view, but decreasing life satisfaction, he was selling off all of the best hours of his life.

The bridge out of the middle was the first 40. First, Max must Get Out of his psychological identification with his profession and he must learn to tell his own unique story. Max must Create His Own Legend. Max's focus changes from being the technical provider of a service to being the owner of business which provides that service. And now, with the mindset of a business owner, Max is free to focus on what will enhance his business, free him from income limits, and allow him to *own* his time again.

The Universe Model was the 20, the map through the Jungle. Max learns the strategic plan that will allow him to tap into the power of Social Media Marketing. He builds the platform upon which The Shift will live.

By shifting a portion of his time away from hourly fee-for-service work and investing that time into the conversion of knowledge, expertise, and experience into information products that can be sold for profit, Max has made the critical transformation.

Through the time invested in the creation of information products, and using those information products as "content" that moves through the online universe, Max is now generating streams of passive income. He can now decrease his fee-for-service hours while building multiple streams of passive income. This allows Max to command a higher rate for the service hours he chooses to provide since he no longer "needs" those client hours. The result is increased income *and* increased discretionary time.

An example from Charlie: My sister, Nancy, taught elementary school for 32.6 years. Hall duty, lunch duty, recess, detention hall, lesson plans, report cards, varicose veins… she did it all.

But do you see how she was trading hours for dollars? What if she were able to teach one full year, record all of it on video, with images, sound, and workbooks, and then simply *play* it for the next 31.6 years while she was off doing something else? And what if she could get someone ELSE to turn on the playback machine!

Do you see how she would have been freed-up to do much more than teach the same material year after year?

Do you see how this applies to YOU?

How often do you give a talk for work or to a local service group based on a topic you know well? Do you record it and get a transcript typed? Do you ever offer that same information to others, others who can benefit from it and pay you for it?

Here is an example from Dr. Marc: One of the things I often did in my psychology practice was work on stress reduction with clients. I was trained in hypnosis and guided imagery, and I used some of these approaches in treatment. I can't claim any great entrepreneurial insight here: the truth is that I found these approaches quite boring to administer despite how effective they could be.

So I developed a series of pre-recorded sessions that I could give to my patients on CD or later sell online. That helped a light bulb go off in my head about how I could suddenly leverage my time with an information product.

This is a mind shift just like the first one. The typical professional is out giving talks and presentations to generate new business – new opportunities to trade time for money. Unless you make The Shift, you will be throwing away golden opportunities. Capture that presentation and make it into a product that is delivered online independent of your time.

This is the powerful leverage that information products create. You create multiple streams of income. And, because the product is a one-time effort in its creation that rewards you many times over, you have just found a way to create passive income. There is no limit to the number of such income streams you can layer onto your business because they do not consume your time on an ongoing basis.

What do you do to become an infopreneur? You **capture** and **package** what you already know and then, as you will see soon, you **market**, **syndicate**, **automate**, and **outsource** what you've produced.

Capture

Living in the digital age is a wonderful thing. In the past, creating photographs, shooting video, and making even basic audio recordings all had associated expenses that quickly started to add up. You had to buy film and have it developed. You needed all kinds of recording media.

But now – now with a few inexpensive devices, you can record to your heart's content knowing that ones and zeros of digital information have no associated costs. You just throw away all the unusable information and keep the best of the best.

Capture as much of what you do in your professional life as you can. Make it a habit. You simply will be amazed at how much great stuff happens that is simply lost in endless passing moments.

When you have capture systems in place and make it a habit to use them often, you develop a mountain of information. Buried within that mountain are veins of gold which you can now mine to develop whole new aspects of your business.

When you provide a service, it is your time that is valuable because of the expertise you have developed through all of your training and experience. When you capture the information that goes into the delivery of that service, you have a product that is valuable to other people. That product no longer requires you to expend your personal time to deliver the value to your customers, clients, and patients.

This is not a substitute for your time. Many people initially fear that they are going to put themselves out of business because they will no longer be needed to deliver their special service.

Information products do not replace services: they enhance them. They exist in addition to the services you provide. Their power really lies in their ability to leverage your time. There are only certain aspects of what you provide that can be captured in a useful way, but where there is a good fit, you can now be in many places at once because this information will live on in the information products you sell. Put your knowledge to work for you without endlessly having to invest your time in the delivery of the same message.

Consider this example: a physician who creates an information product educating patients about the use of proper diet and exercise in the management of diabetes is not replacing his or her skill in the medical management of the disease. That doctor now has a tool that serves multiple functions that enhance the practice.

A video series on diabetes management allows that physician to give or sell to patients something of value. It extends the physician's relationship with that patient because the physician is right there with the patient in the patient's home reinforcing important behavior changes every time the patient hits the play button on the DVD.

Having this product allows the physician to eliminate the drudgery of repeating the same information over and over again, patient after patient. That is not the skillful part of medicine – it is the part that leads to burn out. So this information product leverages time. Ten people can be interacting with the doctor in acquiring important information while the doctor is meeting with one particular patient who requires skilled intervention.

Could the professional just give customers and clients generic information products produced by someone else? Of course, but that would not have nearly the same power.

Let's keep going with the physician example though this applies to most other Professionals just as Max surmised. Let's assume that the American Diabetes Association already has a great video series on diet and exercise. If the doctor gives that out rather than creating a personalized version, there is no personal connection to that doctor's patients. The power of each professional developing unique information products is that the client builds the actual relationship with you as a very specific, unique individual.

The basic information may be the same. But people need the personal relationship in order to stay motivated and really take in that information. That is why when we work with dozens of doctors, there is no competition between the information products that we help them create and develop. These are relationship-building tools whose power comes from the fact that it is you, the professional, that your clients and customers trust, delivering that information in the style that is unique to your personality.

When we say Don't Stand Out – Get Out, perhaps you better understand that you cannot be replaced. You – when you create your own Legend and build relationships that are true to your unique narrative – you have no competition in the marketplace.

So what is it that you need to capture? The answer is: as much as possible.

A digital audio recorder is your best friend. Interview your colleagues about important topics and capture that content. Then set up a very inexpensive video camera and record a little summary describing what that interview is all about. Write up a quick text description of the interview.

Imagine turning your "competition" into a new set of customers. You can capture the most successful business systems and strategies you have developed, package them as we will describe in a moment, and then sell them to your former "competitors." We say *former* because as you make this shift, they will no longer *be* your competitors. They, and everyone else in your profession with an Internet connection, are now part of an exponentially-expanded customer base.

Think back to Allison's accounting colleague who created software for his clients. Having done that, he could now think about creating an information product documenting the step-by-step process he went through to create and market that software product. That is a *new* information product that would be of great value to other accountants (and many other professionals for that matter) who have their own areas of expertise.

As accountants, they are competitors for accounting clients. As infopreneurs, they can not only market to each other, but also collaborate and help market each other's products. We will discuss the world of "affiliate marketing" in a separate ebook available from our website as it is too large a topic to get into here. But let's just say that many people will be amazed to learn that there are online marketers making millions of dollars simply promoting other people's information products.

The physician in our example might finish creating the diet and exercise video series for her diabetic patients. She might then create a step-by-step manual about how she created this video series and market that information product to other physicians across the entire online world.

Anything that you have learned to do that solves a problem that other people are likely to share is a great topic for an information product. The key to getting started is to capture.

Have a colleague shoot video of your next presentation at a meeting or convention. Better yet, have two people shoot from different angles while also capturing an audio recording in case the video does not work well.

In the next section, we discuss how you can take these raw materials and package them into polished information products. You have already done the most important part of the work: you have captured.

What else might you capture? Let's say you are about to meet with a customer, client, or patient. And you know you are about to go through information that you have repeated a million times over the years – you can give this little speech in your sleep. Ask your client if they would be okay if you set up a video camera over his or her shoulder – only you will be on camera. Then with the camera rolling, you talk directly to the client in front of you and provide your valuable information.

You now have a video that has you talking directly to EVERY client. This is something that you can use in your marketing system. You might give away the download of this video in exchange for contact information on your website. Though we will cover more of that in the marketing section, can you see the power of having this material to work with?

The point is that there are endless opportunities for you to capture valuable information in a way that creates almost no new work for you. And by making these small efforts, you start building that mountain that contains veins of gold. If you don't like the outcome, you delete it and do it again with the next client. Eventually, you are going to have one of those moments when you are at the top of your game. And if the camera or audio recorder were not on, that nugget of gold is gone!

It's time to capture!

Package

Now that you have audio, video, and text in raw material form, you mine this gold and create your videos, audio podcasts, and written blog posts.

Today's technology makes all of this very simple and quite affordable. As a professional and business person, you now have amazing technology available right at your fingertips for very little cost. You, as an individual, essentially can own your own newspaper (blog), radio station (podcast, iTunes), and television station (YouTube, Ustream, Livestream).

For almost no expense you can own your own media empire and use it to market yourself and the information products you make available on these platforms.

When Charlie started his video and still photography business in the year 2000, he spent tens of thousands of dollars for equipment. Today, you can get smaller, less-expensive, easier-to-use equipment and software for a fraction of that. And you can then present your work online within minutes.

Let's see how you can package video, audio, and text.

Video

Video is **so** important in today's world both online and off.

Founded in February 2005, YouTube is the world's most popular online video community and it allows people from around the world to connect. Hundreds of millions of videos are watched daily, according to YouTube's own information. And, every minute of every day, more than 20 hours of video are uploaded to YouTube. That's every minute! So it's fair to say that online video is attracting people.

More important to all of us, perhaps, are the demographics which show that YouTube's user base has a broad age range of 18 to 55, evenly divided between males and females, and spanning all geographies. Fifty-one percent of their users visit YouTube weekly or more often, and 52 percent of 18 to 34-year-olds share videos often with friends, schoolmates, and colleagues.

Once you have created the habit of capturing content on video, you have the raw materials that can be edited into everything from a very simple single camera video clip, to a much more elaborate multi-camera shoot with editing that includes graphics and soundtracks. It is all a matter of time and budget. But even the most basic use of video will make all of your marketing efforts jump far out in front of the field. The use of video, more than any other medium, is the fast track to Get Out and Create Your Own Legend. With a total investment of about $150 for a Flip video camera, and software that is already bundled on your computer, you are up and running.

Video delivery from online is so easy these days. At PersonalSuccessMarketing.com we upload our videos to YouTube first, copy the link of the video's location from YouTube, and input that into our website's player and instantly our videos appear for you to watch. We do this for multiple reasons. YouTube gives us direct access to a massive potential audience. YouTube also functions immediately as one of our "planets" in the Universe Model with a URL link right back to our main site. In addition, YouTube is very easy on the budget – it's free.

Videos can be available free (as most of ours are), packaged for online courses, and even put onto DVDs for hardcopy delivery.

The most important part of this is: You Can Only Use It Once You Record It. So get busy with the video camcorder!

None of this is overly complicated or difficult to accomplish. You can select the level of effort and creativity you want to put into this process. Even the most basic video content can be used very effectively in your marketing and in the creation of powerful information products.

You also have the choice of simply capturing the video content and then outsourcing the editing and packaging process. It is a choice of time and budget available. We will discuss this in more detail when we talk about setting up your systems.

Audio Podcasts

Please don't let the term "podcast" confuse you – this just means that you have taken a video or audio file and made it available to people online. And if you think about making it available to someone's iPod, you'll understand the term completely.

With a microphone and free software, you can record podcasts directly into your computer. Like video, you can go from very simple and very inexpensive to setting up a full sound studio. We recommend that you keep it simple and focus on the quality of your information. Studio quality sound is not only unnecessary, it is not what your customers and clients are interested in. It is your expertise and experience that matters.

If YouTube is the headquarters for video online, iTunes is the main location for audio podcasts. Though you can't play the audios from the iTunes website (you must have the files located on your own website – iTunes just provides links to where your audio files are already located), iTunes is a great way to let people know you exist. And, just like YouTube, iTunes does this for FREE!

Audio can also be put on CDs very easily. Every computer made over the past 7 years has CD-burning software included. Once you create your audio file, save it as an MP3 and burn it as an Audio CD or copy the MP3 to a data CD and people can drag and drop the MP3 file directly to their iPod or computer's hard drive.

Blog Posts

The term blog post is, perhaps, a bit unusual. Web-log became weblog, and then was shortened to simply blog (like a diary on your website). And you "post" the weblog to your website.

Thus the term Blog Post.

A blog post is just a written document that appears on your website. They average 500 words on most websites and provide great information in short bursts of text, graphics, and photographs. Type an article in your word processor, copy and paste it into your website's blog software, and publish it once you've edited it.

Posts can also include the audio and video that you've created, and here's why: Google and the other search engines cannot "read" what's in video or audio files, at least not yet. So when you post them to your website, you'll need some text to explain to your website visitor what the audio and video are, *and* you need it there so the search engines can index what you have.

At PersonalSuccessMarketing.com, all of our video and audio podcasts have explanatory text with them. And we also have Foundation Posts that are just text. These are articles that are the foundation for building a great entrepreneurial business.

Think of your blog like a column you read in the newspaper or a monthly feature in a magazine. Only this newspaper or magazine is part of *your* media empire. You determine how often you post. We recommend weekly, monthly at the very least. You can also simply focus on developing the topics and an outline about what you want to cover and then outsource the actual writing and posting to a freelancer. Ever wonder how all those blogs get written every week? We happen to enjoy writing our own, but you don't have to.

The Magic Of Packaging!

Here's where the real fun begins – when you take Video, Audio, and Text and package them all together.

Here's an example.

Let's say you want to market one of your information products.

1. Create a short video about your topic – this should be mostly an introduction or a summary.

2. Record an interview where you describe all the features and benefits and give the "meat" of what people want to hear.
3. Then get a transcript of your MP3 typed and offer that along with your audio file.

You have just created a valuable product. Then write up a blog post that describes what you are offering and put it all on your website. Now *this* is how Video, Audio, and Text come together and it's easy to do!

We have discussed only some of the many types of information products that can be created out of the knowledge, skill, and experience that you already possess. There are many more.

Good old-fashioned book writing still works just fine. And by choosing to go right from your word processor to the web, you can bypass all the joys of traditional publishing and the significant costs that go along with it. An ebook is just a book that a reader purchases online and downloads directly to their computer. Never underestimate the desire for instant gratification.

You can simply decide to write a weekly or monthly blog column and think of it as a year-long book writing process. At the end of the year, you repackage the entire series as an ebook or a traditional book.

Information in the form of the written word, recorded voice, and video presentation can be combined, packaged, and repackaged into many forms. They can be delivered as a single product, delivered as a monthly subscription, or created as a series delivered as a multi-part online course. The only limit is your imagination.

The Shift – Part II: Infopreneur to Infopreneur on Steroids!

Maximillion, on his way up to The Dragon's lair, caught a glimpse of The Summit, up there in a haze of clouds. But it was merely a subliminal image to his mind. He had urgent work to do, and he had to head back to The Kingdom, save the day, and establish himself in his profession.

Max picks up on that image and, what was subliminal to Maximillion, breaks through and awakens within Max a much more powerful desire. Max wants more than to be just "relatively successful" at the price of selling off the best hours of his life, hoping to be able to get to the meaning of his life. Well, someday, he hopes.

Max wakes up and realizes that he needs to Get Out, he needs to get back on track to The Summit of his career so that he has the time and space to define what PersonalSuccess means to him, to define his DreamDestination. Max needs the steroids of automation.

Max is ready to take the chance to produce information products that convert his thoughts into cash, without the earnings-ceiling of trading hours for dollars. Hopefully, your brain is getting excited about the opportunity to break free of the barriers created by limited time and limited geography that are created by only providing direct service in your business.

But how are you going to stay up on all those purchases of your information products? You are busy, you don't have time to sell your books, CDs, ebooks, and more… In fact, maybe you're not yet cured of your aversion to the concept of "sales."

What if you could automate all of this? Can you see it? People purchasing information from you 24 hours a day and all you need to do is spend the money that they pay you (because even collecting the money is automated and deposits automatically appear in your bank account)?

It's not as simple as popping up a website, plugging in your products, and telling the shopping cart where to deposit your money but when you see the steps, when you have a system, and when you know what to do, you'll wonder why you didn't do this YEARS ago!

This is where you are going to build an automated, online-delivery system. This is where your income really breaks away from time and geography. This is how a one-time effort is leveraged to the point that you are rewarded many, many times over for every hour you invest.

This is key to The Shift: instead of selling your time, you now invest it. And just like an invested dollar grows through the magic of compound interest, time invested in creating an information product and putting it on an automated platform creates more time.

Let's say you are a specialist seeing 40 patients a week. Your income can only expand in a linear fashion. Add one more patient a week and you get to collect one more hourly fee. Now let's say that rather than doing that, you drop down to 39 patients a week and invest that one hour a week into writing an ebook in an area of your expertise.

So for the time it takes you to create that ebook, you have lost one hour of income a week. But once you finish the project and set it up on the kind of system we will show you how to build, you have regained your time. But now your ebook sales grow week by week as your marketing platform puts it out in front of a larger and larger audience. Your income from that one hour a week investment can increase at an exponential rate.

Because of that, you might look at this from the point of view that your information product has just bought you back that hour. And now you are getting paid *not* to work that extra hour. You might find that you like that. You might decide to keep buying back more of your hours the same way. And what might really knock your socks off is discovering that by making The Shift, you earn more by working less.

Market

At PersonalSuccess Marketing, we have both a simple way of looking at marketing and a more complex, strategic view. We have already presented to you our Universe Model of Social Media Marketing in an overview form. Other materials that teach you the tactical use of specific tools are available for you on our website, in additional information products, and at our LiveEvents. For the moment, let's take a look at the simple, underlying principle: marketing is about building relationships. And you have been marketing all of your life.

This is why in discussing Get Out, we focused on changing your mindset of *being* your profession to focus on the concept that you are the *marketer* of your professional service. And now, we simply extend that notion to say that as you develop information products based upon your area of expertise, you become the marketer of professional information.

You also begin to have the freedom to decide whether you will develop information products in addition to the services you continue to offer, or decide that these new income streams will begin to replace direct-service hours as you buy back your time.

As you develop information products, we will show you how to use some of them purely as relationship-building tools. And as an aside, let's point out that video is a particularly powerful vehicle for doing just that. When people "interact" with you on video, they begin to develop a personal connection with you without your ever having met them. Just look at the kind of fan response that celebrities get.

When you speak directly to the camera, you are making eye contact with people and speaking directly to them. It is a very powerful tool.

As a marketer, one of the most important things that you will do is build your list. If marketing is relationship building at its core, then you have to start the process by connecting and exchanging contact information so that you can begin (or continue) to develop a conversation.

Information products are a great tool to help you achieve this list-building goal. Think for a moment about the last time you invited people over for dinner. You offered your guests something of value. They sat down and had a great meal and conversation. Perhaps some of them brought a bottle of wine, something for dessert, or maybe flowers. Why? Because human beings are hardwired to respond to each other in a reciprocal fashion. Reciprocity is a very powerful reflex – you do something for me and I instantly feel a sense of obligation to respond in kind.

Information products can function as a core element in the marketing of both the service end of your business and the marketing of additional information products. You can use an information product like a special report (or audio or video interview) and offer it on your website as a quid pro quo. "You are welcome to download this free product in exchange for your name and email address so that we can begin, or continue, to have a conversation about what is important to you." You give them something and they respond by giving you their name and email address, and you build your list!

In the same way that it is polite to show up to a dinner party with an offering as a thank-you for the meal and hospitality, your marketing can include an offering of value to your online guests. If your visitor recognizes the value in your offer, you will bring out a natural feeling of reciprocity. A name and an email address is not much to ask for if you have done a good job of demonstrating the value of your offer.

This is one of the many beautiful qualities of information products. You market them by giving away free samples of your work and in return ask simply for permission to have a conversation about the additional value you have to offer your customers and clients.

However, the real power of this approach – the marriage of information products and the online delivery systems – is that the entire process runs on autopilot. You invest your time once in the creation of the *product*, and you invest your time once in the creation of your online *systems*. But you generate ongoing streams of income that can indefinitely reward you for those initial investments. The marketing runs on autopilot. The sales process runs on autopilot. The delivery of the product to the customer runs on autopilot.

This is what we mean when we say that making The Shift from professional to infopreneur is a way to buy back your time. You have just created a marketing system that delivers passive income to you. In fact, it is passive, residual income in that it keeps paying you as a byproduct just as surely as the royalties on a hit song would.

And what are you to do with the time you have now bought back? Well, in truth, anything that you want. However, we are going to suggest that you repeat the process and create the next information product that becomes the next stream of income.

Create the next product and feed it into the front end of your marketing machine and then enjoy that second income stream. Then continue repeating this cycle until you have layered enough streams of passive income, buying back more and more of your time, taking you out of the center of the business, and freeing you from the TimeTrap Plateau.

Once you have captured and packaged information, it's time to put the infopreneur side of your business on steroids. In Chapter 14, we introduced you to the overview of the Universe Model of Social Media Marketing. This is the platform that will take your information product and send it through the "universe" of the online world.

We looked at how energy flows through this system with your main website as the hub of a marketing solar system. When you create an ebook, for example, and you set it up on your main website for sale, we will show you how to create a brief video summarizing your new product, write a blog post about it, and record an audio podcast about it.

You will then launch these components off like a three-stage rocket and allow it to travel through this universe. Using these simple bits of text, audio, and video you are able to set in motion a sequence that moves links through from the stars, to the planets, and all driving traffic home to the sun (your Money Site) at the center of your solar system. This draws the traffic back to the location where people can purchase and download your ebook.

Syndicate

As luck would have it, the online jungle is already filled with innovators who have developed some amazing tools. While this is not the place for us to go into them in great detail, it is important to understand that they are available to put your marketing machine into hyperdrive.

Let's just take one example. One of the ways to drive traffic through your online Universe is for you to create accounts at other people's blog sites and routinely provide your content on their websites. Of course you include a link that ties that content back to your Money Site. The more you do this, the more links you create, and the more your site increases in relevance to the almighty search engines that are constantly indexing the entire web.

Now, that would be very time consuming, indeed. Lucky for us, we live in a world full of entrepreneurs, and where a problem is identified, there is often a clever person or two who have found a ready-made solution for you.

On our website, you will find recommendations for the solutions that we use regularly because we have already put them to work in our marketing machine. One of these is a powerhouse system to syndicate your video content. It is one of the many reasons that we focus on using video in our own marketing and you can find more information at <u>PersonalSuccess Marketing Tools We Recommend</u>.

With the "touch of a button" you can take a video you have created to promote the important information on your website and launch it out into the Universe. This tool uses scores of sites throughout the Internet that you set up once and it uses over and over. When you press the button, your video, like magic, is pushed out to all these other sites, immediately creating hundreds of links right back to the hub of your marketing system – your Money Site.

This is but one example of what we mean by shifting from infopreneur to infopreneur-on-steroids! We have quite a few different types of steroids in our medicine chest that we have tested and validated for you.

Automate (With Systems to Free Your Time)

At PersonalSuccess Marketing, one of the core dimensions to our business model is that we spend time on a task long enough to map it out in very specific detail. Your business is full of parts that are endlessly-repeating cycles. Any cycle that you can identify can be mapped out as a series of sequential steps.

Once you have tested a sequence to ensure that you have captured all of the essential components, you can map out the system for the completion of that cycle. If you do this with sufficient clarity, you can then hand that system off to have someone else complete it while you step back to monitor the results.

This is why a massive enterprise like the McDonald's empire is essentially run on a day-to-day basis by teenagers. Every component of a McDonald's franchise has been systematized and put into manuals and task sheets so that anyone can complete the tasks. People come and go, but the *systems* are forever keeping all the gears in sync.

Some of these cycles can be completed through the use of technology. Others require human input. But the key element to understand is that in *your* business, you need to step out of being responsible for their completion. Ideally, you don't even want to be responsible for the immediate supervision of that system. You want to define the key outcome variables, those data points that you keep your eye on. You can then sit back to look at the flashing lights on the master-control board of your business. The numbers tell you whether or not everything is running smoothly.

You define each layer of your business, develop the sequential system for its smooth operation, and then hand that component off. You then step up to the next layer, develop it, systematize it, and hand that off. At each step, you define the numbers – the statistics, the metrics – that will allow you to glance at a report and know that all systems are operating well. Conversely, you will know exactly when there is a system breakdown and where the problem lies in the chain.

On the PersonalSuccess Marketing website, we maintain a resource list where you will find numerous automation systems that we use on a regular basis in our business, and we can therefor recommend them to you as well. Click here: PersonalSuccess Marketing Tools We Recommend

Outsource

Before some folks get up-in-arms, nationalistic, and patriotic, let's be clear that by "outsourcing" we do not mean that you have to ship your tasks overseas (though some people certainly do). Outsourcing simply means having someone else take over portions of your workflow and complete these tasks for you.

One of the most important reasons for taking the time to automate and create systems is so that you can hand off aspects of the work flow to other parts of your team. When it comes to outsourcing, the Internet has once again changed everything.

In 2005, Thomas Friedman published **The World Is Flat**. In this fascinating examination of how technology has made the world into one highly-interconnected place, Friedman discusses how we have gone from a world dominated by national borders and governments, to a world dominated by multinational corporations, and finally to a world of global freelancers for hire.

Just about any portion of your work flow that does not require physical presence at your immediate, geographic location can now be handled by a virtual member of your team. By doing so, you keep the infrastructure of your business lean and nimble. Outsourcing allows you to run your business based on projects. You scale up and scale down as needed without the problems of hiring, firing, and managing a large scale payroll.

You are not only leveraging your time, but you are leveraging economies of scale, and taking advantage of variations in currency and cost of living in different parts of the country or even different parts of the world. Chances are you can get the work done cheaper, faster, and by someone with the exact skill sets you require. In **The 4-Hour Workweek**, Tim Ferriss makes the comment that life gets pretty interesting when you earn your money in dollars, live on pesos, and pay your workers in rupees.

Now we may not all want to pull up roots and practice "geographic arbitrage" the way Ferriss does; however, we know from personal experience that a very great deal of what we have described here in these pages can be systematized, automated, and outsourced, leaving you to be the business owner, the creative force that drives the enterprise.

At PersonalSuccess Marketing, we are continually building the network of people that make up our team. There are no employees, only freelancers and joint venture partners. We have parts of our writing team locally on the east coast, another part in California, and another team in Texas. We have virtual project managers in Bangalore, India.

Across the United States and around the world, there are individuals, small firms, and very large companies that can provide nearly any service that your business requires, all without having to manage the overhead issues that go along with payroll, benefit packages, office space – the list goes on.

If you visit a website like Elance.com (and this is only one example among many – please see our ebook on Outsourcing for much more detailed information about resources as well as all the ins and outs of the outsourcing process), you can post any project, large or small, and have people bid on the work you need done.

You can review their references right there by looking at ratings and comments provided by that provider's previous clients. You can specify and negotiate your terms, and you can even arrange to have a neutral third party hold funds in escrow until you authorize their release after the work has been completed to your satisfaction.

Outsourcing this way allows you to organize your business around specific projects. And using well defined systems, outsourcing allows your business to scale up as rapidly as you need as your business grows in volume.

Dealing with the creation of information products lends itself perfectly to this model. Almost every aspect of this process can be handled remotely. Digital information moves around the world at the speed of light passing through fiber optic cables. In fact, Tom Friedman in his book examines how in many ways this outsourced world owes its success to the dotcom bust. It was at the height of that bubble that huge sums of money were invested in undersea fiber optic cables linking the United States to India. While the companies that made those investments came and went, the cables remained and became the infrastructure for a different online explosion.

Some very quick online research allows you to have maximum competition for your projects, and through that competition you are able to keep costs in check. This is the free market system on steroids. By searching several freelance sites, you can easily establish the going rate for the different tasks and projects you need to keep on budget.

Outsourcing becomes a critical component in the buying back your time.

The Wealth of Time

This is the journey to The Summit, and from that summit you are free to begin making that shift from success to significance. Max's Dilemma has found its resolution. He has built the bridge over the moat that got him stranded. He has moved to the edge of the plateau and equipped himself for the jungle expedition. With his map and the proper tools, Max has followed the Universe Model of Social Media Marketing and has made a series of shifts and gone from entrepreneur to infopreneur.

And what is his reward? Time. Max has claimed the wealth of time. Max stands at The Summit, supported by multiple streams of passive income being generated by the information products that he has developed. He is able to manage his business at arms length by using automation through both technology and outsourcing sequences of work to a small army of freelancers. Max is now free to reinvest his time into what has true meaning to him.

This is the PersonalSuccess Marketing 40/20/40 System in action. We have discovered an interesting phenomenon along the way in our own journey. We developed this system to break free from our own versions of the TimeTrap Plateau. In working to Get Out, Create Our Own Legend, Master the Online Jungle, and climb to The Summit, we have focused on mapping the journey. Like The Stranger's father in Maximillion's Tale, we drew the map of the territory for our own benefit. And along the way, we discovered many, many weary travelers trapped within Max's Dilemma. Our goal is now to share that map with all those who can benefit from it.

The map is far more detailed than we can fully describe in the pages of this book. You will need to follow the path back to the online origin of this book (PersonalSuccessMarketing.com) where we are building a community for highly-skilled professionals who have followed the old, flawed map to the plateau. The ultimate goal of this journey is to arrive at your DreamDestination. This map cannot define that destination for you because it is unique to you. But it can take you to a space where there is sufficient time, a wealth of time, that will allow you to define your DreamDestination.

Section IV – Where IS My Summit?

Chapter 16 – DreamDestination

Why?

PersonalSuccess Marketing gets you to your DreamDestination. We begin right where you are – you are a very busy professional stuck on the TimeTrap Plateau, surrounded by the moat created by running endlessly in circles around yourself at the center of your business. We begin by helping you to build a bridge over that moat so that you don't just stand out, you Get Out.

We then meet you at the edge of the Online Jungle where we outfit you with your personal strategic map, provide you with the Universe Model of Social Media Marketing, and help you use the online tools that allow you to conquer this Jungle. We then help you make several critical shifts to begin systematically buying back your time so that you never again find yourself stuck on that TimeTrap Plateau. Together we can build new streams of income by capturing your expertise, packaging it into the form of information products, and blasting it out into the online universe.

Now the knowledge, experience, and expertise that you have spent years of your life developing begin to reward you many times over. You will never again simply have to trade your time for money. You begin to regain your true wealth, the wealth of time.

But before you even begin this journey, we ask you to look up. Look up above the canopy of the Jungle to see The Summit – the place you thought you were heading for before you became trapped on this plateau. We remind you that the reason you headed into the jungle in the first place was so that you could get back on the right path, the one that leads up to the summit of your professional career.

But why? Why are we going up there in the first place?

"Why" is the most important question of all. Actually, you are heading to The Summit to discover your Why. At The Summit you gain a grand perspective upon this entire landscape – the real purpose of your career, all your hard work. Why did you set out on this journey in the first place? What was the dream? What was your DreamDestination? The sum total of your work is the quest to answer that question, because from the height of The Summit, you can clearly see your DreamDestination.

What exactly is your DreamDestination? That is something that we cannot answer for you fully.

Our goal is to pave the way to The Summit. The Summit is where you have moved up and over The Jungle's canopy, up to an altitude where your vision is clear and you can survey the entire landscape.

Our goal is to take you to a place where you are no longer bogged down and tangled in the marketing of your business and you have moved off the plateau where you were trapped in the center of your business, running in circles and digging an ever deeper moat around yourself.

Our goal is to take you to a place where you *own* your time again and have the freedom to sit down to define your DreamDestination.

At our week-long PersonalSuccess Summit™ – where we take you straight through the Jungle and head right to *your* summit – you will go on a retreat from the day-to-day activities of your life. We *really* will head out into the jungle (though ours will be at an exclusive resort location!). You will work intensively with our team of experts.

At our PersonalSuccess Summits you will become part of an InnerCore Mastermind Group. This group of 10-12 people will become your personal board of advisors as you all finally work together to break free. Together, you will help each other dream a bigger dream as you do the work of defining your DreamDestination.

Every year at our PersonalSuccess Summits we take our InnerCore group right through the 40/20/40 System. By the end of this Summit, you will Get Out: you will have Created Your Own Legend and defined a new professional identity that will forever enable you to break free from the center of your business. You will focus the Universe Model of Social Media Marketing, and by the end of this Summit, you will be Master of the Online Jungle. You will make The Shift that will unleash you upon the world as an Infopreneur on Steroids!

The PersonalSuccess Summit is not for everyone, and we recognize that. In fact, there is only room for a group of 10-12 at a time.

For others, we can hear you clearly: "Dr. Marc and Charlie, it's been YEARS since I slew my dragon, earned my degree, set up my business and then life happened! I got married, had children who are growing up nicely and heading toward college, but what's this talk about a Summit? Isn't it ok that my life is going well, we're happy, and I seem to be providing a nice life for me and my family?"

It is PERFECTLY OK! Yes.

A lot of people want what YOU already have and would be thrilled with exactly what you described.

However…

- if you've lost sight of where you thought you were going when you headed off after college or graduate school
- if you're running in circles faster and faster just to stay where you are
- if you want to take some time away from your business or practice, but feel everything will grind to a halt if you do
- if you're wondering what real value is in your business since you seem to do everything and everything revolves around you
- if you're looking ahead to retirement (or simply want to break away from what you are doing now) and wonder what you can sell your business for, once you are no longer the major producer
- if you've seen the future and realize that you have to change the way you run your business so that you will be able to *have* a life after you no long run it…

… then we should chat further.

Your DreamDestination is different from ours. Only *you* can decide what is right for you. Maybe you want to:

- travel the world for 6 months, photographing all the beautiful cities you studied in history class
- rent an RV, stopping in remote locations for weeks at a time just to appreciate life and people
- cruise the Caribbean, the Mediterranean, and around Alaska and want your income to keep flowing in while you do it

- start a new business (or several) to help other people overcome challenges they face
- take a few steps back from running your present business so you don't have to work so hard, knowing someone else can run it day-to-day
- rest, relax, enjoy your grandchildren, or play some golf or tennis
- move to a warmer climate to enjoy boating or move to the mountains where you can ski any time you want to
- keep earning at a high level as you commit your time to a cause that grabs your heart and spirit
- and so many more.

You are unique, as your Legend can attest. The desires you have for your life are uniquely your own.

Being stuck on a plateau not knowing how to move forward isn't how life has to be, as our material has demonstrated. No matter WHAT you want, there's a path ready to be cut to get you there.

First, you have to SEE The Summit again, and then we can work together to get you the shortest, most-direct path to it.

So… this part of your story has yet to be written. Imagine what life will be like at your DreamDestination. Think about it, dream about it, let yourself imagine how great life will be for you and your family and then we'll help you get there.

Dare to dream. Close your eyes to see in your mind's eye what awaits you at your DreamDestination. Yours is unique to you. But dare to dream, and then dream much bigger. If you truly owned your time, the true measure of wealth, how would you choose to spend it?

Don't settle for a simple answer. Grow the image in your mind. Let it disrupt the status quo. Everything that really matters begins in your mind.

There is a character in the book **Peaceful Warrior**, Socrates. Soc tells his student, Dan, "Take out the trash." And he taps Dan on the forehead, explaining that by trash he means all the thoughts that get in the way of seeing, really seeing, things as they are.

Do you see with your eyes? Or do you see with your thoughts, with your preconceived notions of how things should or ought to be?

Dare to be unreasonable in imagining your DreamDestination. As someone once said, it is not reasonable for someone to be able to flip a switch and fill a room with light. It's not reasonable for a massive hulk of metal with several hundred people on board to be able to fly through the air.

These things exist because creative people imagined the impossible. Then they worked like crazy to force reality to bend to their vision. They used their minds to change present reality, bring into existence something that simply did not exist prior to that.

What are the reasonable rules in your life right now that shut you down from dreaming much, much bigger? It is your mind that decides either to keep you on the Plateau or head for The Summit. Those who choose the path to the summit have no special talents. They are not smarter, not richer, and not more beautiful than you are.

They have mastered a few basic but crucial skills. They dream big, and they *take action* to realize those dreams. It is not that they lack the same fears we all experience, but they have learned to take action in the face of those fears.

Dare. After all, you are already a DragonSlayer.

If you are a mid-career, mid-life professional then it is time for you to take action. It really is now or never. Don't torture yourself: either decide to get comfortable on the plateau and let go of the frustration *or* decide that the time is now and that your PersonalSuccess Summit awaits.

If you are ready to take on the 40/20/40 System, then now is the time to get busy. Your first step is to visit our website at PersonalSuccessMarketing.com to register in the upper right hand corner of any page. It is time for us to exchange contact information and start building a relationship.

Dare to dream.

And if you are going to dream, then dare to dream big. Define your DreamDestination. Use all of your senses to bring the vision into reality. In your mind's eye, paint a three-dimensional landscape and then paint yourself right into the middle of it.

Remember Maximillion's Tale. His lighter, stronger armor did not come from his adding the special stuff to the existing formula used in the smithy to make steel. It was only when he combined the Dragon's scales with basic elements like earth and water that the transformation was possible.

You and we – we all share the same basic emotions. Conquer The Dragon: that is our intrinsic fear in the face of change and The Unknown. Do it anyway. Do it despite your fears.

It is not the technology alone that will take you to your DreamDestination. It is your mind having such clarity of vision that you will say, "Oh, yes, of course I can get there. I can see my path clearly."

Move farther and farther out from the center of your business. Use your new-found freedom to define and pursue what matters most deeply to you in your life.

Charlie on how TimeFreedom leads From Success To Significance:

One of my joys of working with entrepreneurs from around the country is that I get to hear stories about how their TimeFreedom allows them to spend their lives doing exactly what they choose to do. No longer trapped into selling their time for the dollars needed to survive, they have new-found freedom to create exciting and fulfilling ventures.

Time is the true currency, as we've written in this book, and once it's available in sufficient quantities, SummitMasters spend it in ways most people only dream about.

We each have our own Summit and our own DreamDestination, that important place where we yearn to go when our day-to-day needs are taken care of *and* we have enough time to enjoy life and give back to others.

Let me tell you two stories and then tell you what Dr. Marc and I are doing.

Bill Books It Big

As a long-time, very-active member of the Glazer-Kennedy Insider's Circle (GKIC-Philly), I purchased 10 copies of Bill Glazer's Best-Selling Book, **Outrageous Advertising That's Outrageously Successful**, when Bill attended one of our chapter meetings. The book is great (jammed with terrific marketing and advertising techniques to zoom your success right to the top) and by purchasing 10 copies at that meeting I paved my way to attend Bill's big event in Orlando, Florida on the same topic.

In Orlando as the meeting began, Bill told of his deep commitment to Junior Achievement and how it is a partnership of the business community, educators, and volunteers. They all work to inspire young people to dream big and reach their potential (and that sure rings true with what we are all about here at PersonalSuccess Marketing). Students are taught key concepts of work readiness, entrepreneurship, and financial literacy.

And as Bill brought some of his local leadership to the stage, he presented them with a check for $100,000 from the sale of his book. ONE HUNDRED THOUSAND DOLLARS! That will help a lot of junior achievers!

The audience rose as one, cheering. Bill left his TimeTrap Plateau years ago and now spends his time both as the president of Glazer-Kennedy supporting entrepreneurs and business leaders as they succeed *and* as a committed supporter of educating our next generation through his involvement with Junior Achievement.

Bill has reached his DreamDestination. And if you would like to join him by supporting Junior Achievement, please go to Junior Achievement to donate. Be sure to tell them that PersonalSuccess Marketing and Bill Glazer sent you!

Mike and Vivian Reach Out – Way Out

At Bill Glazer's Orlando Outrageous Advertising conference, I experienced Mike Koenigs as he presented a dynamic demonstration. Mike spoke for about 50 minutes from the stage, spending the first 45 minutes telling us why internet video marketing is so important to our success. It was only in the last five minutes that he told us about his wizard of a product (Traffic Geyser – To Learn More, Click Here!) that takes videos and quickly distributes them throughout the Internet, building your rankings in Google and the other search engines, driving more buyers to your main website. I signed us up for Traffic Geyser and we've been thrilled with the results.

One of the bonuses for signing up with Traffic Geyser that day was that I was able to attend the Traffic Geyser "FirePower Super Summit" in San Diego two months later. Bill Glazer spoke. So did Brian Tracy. But for *me* the biggest impact came from Mike himself.

Mike is a *very* sharp businessperson in addition to being a video-marketing champion. His mind is so sharp and his insights to people sitting in "hot seats," where they received advice from a small panel of experts, was worth tens of thousands of extra dollars to the participants *and* to each of us in the audience who were smart enough to see how what was said to those on stage applied to each of us as well.

Traffic Geyser isn't Mike's first huge success – by selling a previous business he was able to put away enough money so that he didn't have to worry about paying for the necessities of life, even though he now makes seven figures from his business ventures. Mike learned that to Get Out of the TimeTrap-Plateau mentality would open his life to many more successes… and so it has.

And here's where the story gets *really* good. Mike introduced his wife, Vivian Glyck, who played a video about the **Just Like My Child Foundation** which she founded to transform humanity by empowering women and children to achieve their full potential through improved Health Care, Education, and Microenterprise. In an approach she calls "deep development," they empower communities, village by village, to create their own long-term solutions in rural Uganda.

Vivian explains that becoming a mother didn't just open her heart to the needs of their son, Zak, but as so often happens, it opened her heart to the needs and concerns of mothers and children all around the world. She saw that the world is really just one community and realized that taking care of oneself means heeding one's calling, without hesitation or deliberation.

Talking about the children she is able to help, she quotes Brad Pitt who said, "You want to gather up handfuls of them and bring them home."

There wasn't a dry eye in the large room when Vivian's video was over, and we jumped to our feet to applaud her efforts. Then she thanked Mike for all his business success and the freedom he now has that allows him to spend time helping her with this important cause.

We jumped again to our feet applauding Mike. SHE teared up. HE teared up. WE teared up. And as I wrote in a Thank You note to Mike (for such a great weekend with him), I would have loaned him my handkerchief, but I was using it.

Mike is *living* on his DreamDestination and having a HUGE impact with entrepreneurs whose business successes multiply through his Traffic Geyser, with his latest creation, presently called Voice FollowUp, and through his own efforts to help Vivian in living on *her* DreamDestination.

If you would like to join me in helping the Just Like My Child Foundation – Click Here To Donate! And in the "How Did You Hear About Just Like My Child Foundation" box, please send my love to Vivian and tell her you heard about her work through PersonalSuccess Marketing. And then be sure to sign up for their newsletter and stay involved!

Dr. Marc and Charlie Follow The Lead Of Bill And Mike

Both Bill Glazer and Mike Koenigs are educating children through their efforts. Dr. Marc and I began our partnership with a stated mission of donating 10% of the profits to worthy causes.

Dr. Marc has always been focused on helping his community through his work as a clinical psychologist, first working with brain-injured patients and then spending many years working with cancer patients. Many of his patients lacked insurance coverage for psychological support services, and Dr. Marc worked with people on a sliding scale and pro bono to help them cope. He also worked with some forward-thinking oncology physicians who subsidized psychological services for their patients because they were committed to treating people and not just their diseases. This work also led Dr. Marc to various fund-raising activities for the American Cancer Society.

In addition to my donating photography services for my own church, a local synagogue, a local theater, and a local children's theater, I have been able to travel with our church's middle school kids on annual Mission Trips as we fed the hungry, helped the homeless, and cared for children who need a loving spirit in their lives. Sleeping on hard, wooden church floors for a week-at-a-time never felt so good.

And now more: with the energy of Bill Glazer, Mike Koenigs, and so many others fresh in our hearts and minds, Dr. Marc and I will donate 10% of the dollars we make on the sale of this book to City Year, which unites young people of all backgrounds for a year of full-time service, giving them skills and opportunities to change the world.

As tutors, mentors, and role models, these diverse young leaders help children stay in school and on track, and transform schools and communities across the United States, as well as through international affiliates in Johannesburg, South Africa, and London,

England. Just as important, during their year of service, corps members develop civic-leadership skills they can use throughout a lifetime of community service.

Major corporations and businesses participate in their mission by serving as strategic partners, team sponsors, and national leadership sponsors. Together they're building a citizen-service movement that is larger than their organizations, their own lifetimes, and themselves.

I first learned about City Year through my daughter, Stacie Finnegan, who is part of their national staff in Boston. And the more I learned about their energy, dedication, and life-changing efforts for students, the more I wanted us to be involved.

We also pledge publicly through this book that we will provide, at no fee, places for young people (juniors and seniors in high school plus college-age students – *especially* those who were part of the corps for City Year) to join our LiveEvents to learn about entrepreneurship, escape the TimeTrap Plateau, before they get stuck there, and Create Their Own Legends so they can Get Out from the crowd of people doing activities similar to their own businesses.

So, thank you for investing in yourself and contributing, indirectly, to City Year by purchasing this book. If you would like to join us by contributing directly to City Year – Click Here!

Now It's YOUR Turn – Your DreamDestination Is Waiting

Maximillion and Katherine surged up the mountain to the dragon's lair but couldn't take the time to journey the rest of the way to the summit. Oh... they were successful at their mission. They slew the dragon, and rescued the kingdom, but did they really live "happily ever after"?

Max and Kate woke up one day and found themselves surrounded by a moat created by racing around in circles to keep up in their businesses – stranded upon the TimeTrap Plateau, surrounded by the Online Jungle.

Yet, they saw that there was a better way – a way to bridge the moat, journey through the Online Jungle using the Universe Model of Social Media Marketing, and make The Shift which allowed them to separate their knowledge and expertise from their hourly efforts. They learned to own their time again by creating multiple streams of passive income.

Max recognized that the summit that Maximillion had only glimpsed was the key to his success. He understood that once there, he could discover his DreamDestination.

Now it's your turn. We've peeled back the canopy of the Jungle to show you the summit and tell you how to get to your DreamDestination. Since we see what we look for and we've shown you a lot here, we hope you are ready to set out on this journey, head for The Summit, and find your true DreamDestination.

It's up to you. The path is clear and the time is now.

Now, set out for YOUR DreamDestination and go from Success To Significance as well!

The journey of a thousand miles begins with a single step. Your next step is to join us at PersonalSuccessMarketing.com and become a part of a growing community dedicated to your PersonalSuccess. Then we look forward to sharing even more with you, using our website as the hub of PersonalSuccess Marketing.

Now is your time. Time to dream big and begin your journey. And we're here to help!

Hey... Don't just sit there – Get Out! Why are you still reading this book? Go to our website now to register! Start this journey, and we will see you at The Summit.

About the Authors

Charlie Seymour Jr has really had fun since receiving his MBA from The Wharton School of the University of Pennsylvania and BA from Tufts University.

He sold $247,368,657.97 in personal real estate sales and more than $1 billion through his marketing leadership skills; ran professional theaters in Princeton, NJ and St. Louis, MO; operated his own photography/video production company; consulted about (and uses) Web 2.0 technology (especially blogging, podcasting, video production, and Facebook); directed musical theater (in his "spare" time); and now runs PersonalSuccess Marketing with his business partner, Dr. Marc Kossmann. Charlie is also an Advisor for ParentalWisdom.com, helps the youth of his church in annual work-camp trips, and photographs each production at two local theaters.

At the heart of all of this Charlie has always known he's a marketer, whether it was helping business professionals explode their success in their businesses, getting theater productions produced at several theaters, selling major real estate along the East Coast of the United States, or running his own online businesses. And hand-in-hand with marketing is his love for people, helping them succeed while focusing attention on them when they do.

Charlie recently studied the buying habits of Baby Boomers and loved one phrase to describe many of his generation, "We've gone from Success To Significance in what drives us. We have the things and now want to be sure to leave our mark ON the world (and on at least one other person IN this world)." Charlie embodies that.

Charlie is the father of two beautiful, talented, and grown daughters (Stacie and Liz) who enrich his life in everything they do. He lives outside of Philadelphia in Wallingford, PA USA with his wife, Pam, two cats, a dog, 7 computers, and 8 cameras!

Find out more about Charlie at his LinkedIn Profile.

Dr. Marc Kossmann is a clinical psychologist, Tae Kwon Do black belt, motorcycle-riding entrepreneur who enjoys helping other people succeed.

Once Dr. Marc spent nine days living life by the rules of Buddhist monks with no talking, reading, writing, or eye contact. The goal was to AVOID thinking and just experience, but it was an adventure that helped him see the mind as a fluid, ever-changing process. A process that can get stuck in loops where habits are revealed as one of the most powerful forces of nature.

Trained originally as a neuropsychologist, he went from working in brain-injury rehabilitation centers to focusing on work with cancer patients as part of a multidisciplinary oncology treatment team. While Dr. Marc still treats patients one day a week in his Havertown, PA office and is an Adjunct Professor of Psychology at Rosemont College, he now specializes in entrepreneurship and marketing – marketing that helps get mid-career, mid-life professionals off their business plateaus and directed back to the summits (and their

DreamDestinations) they were aimed at when they earned their degrees.

Dr. Marc saw early-on in his career that while professionals are trained intensively in their "technical skills," they almost never learn anything about marketing and running a business. Together with Charlie, he is now dedicated to helping professionals change.

Dr. Marc lives with his wife, Deb (also a clinical psychologist), and two exceptional cats just outside of Philadelphia, PA USA.

Find out more about Dr. Marc at his LinkedIn Profile.

What Is PersonalSuccess Marketing?

PersonalSuccess Marketing:

Dr. Marc and Charlie made the decision to team up to form PersonalSuccess Marketing as a part of their new company, Online Direct Marketing, LLC, after meeting twice a month over several years (in a business development group) and discussing their mutual passion for marketing and business development.

PersonalSuccess Marketing is the chemical reaction that results from locking an entrepreneurially-focused clinical psychologist and a marketing-crazed MBA in a room for too long. Together, they are determined to show you how the second half of your career is where you can break free and head for the summit you saw when you earned your degree.

For the mid-career, mid-life professional who feels stuck on a plateau and doesn't know how to get off, it's a step-by-step learning process to help you head for the summit of your career. And we have packaged this information in several formats for you depending upon your preference.

You can spend time on our website (PersonalSuccessMarketing.com) and get to know us, interact with us, and figure out if you like what we are doing. Clearly we are not all things to all people – there is a very specific group of people with whom we want to have a conversation. And we trust that by reading our blog posts, listening to our podcasts, and watching our videos, these folks will easily recognize themselves.

We have a series of books, ebooks, and how-to-style DVD courses for people who are do-it-yourself types. We pack as much information as possible into these products so that the self-motivated professional can take that information and run with it. For those who want a little more accountability, assistance, and structure, we have online-course formats with webinars and teleseminars to guide you along the way.

For those who learn best in person, we offer weekend retreats a few times a year where people come to get to know us better in person and learn what we have to offer in detail. We also offer special package discounts on many of the products and services we have available.

Twice a year we hold intensive-training LiveEvents. These are some pretty tightly-focused, boot-camp-style training sessions where people dig into the skills and strategies needed to master the Online Jungle, break free, and really define the DreamDestination that they see from the summit of their career path. We show people exactly what to do and how to do it. And at these events, we provide people with PersonalSuccess Maps and PersonalSuccess Manuals that allow them to transform their businesses over the next six months.

While we do a limited amount of direct consulting ourselves, we train and develop what we refer to as our PersonalSuccess Guides. These are our specialists who work one-on-one and in group formats with people who want a more hands-on level of help in retooling themselves for the second half of their careers. Our PersonalSuccess Guides are highly-trained consultants who work their way up through a three-level ranking system with us. And while most people coming to us want to transform their *own* businesses, some people are looking for a new career path and join us as PersonalSuccess Guides.

But by far our favorite activity out of all the fun stuff we are doing has to be our PersonalSuccess Summits. These are the expeditions that drive straight through the Jungle and head right to *your* summit. These are for a very select group of 10-12 people who have the means and the motivation to go straight to the top.

We assemble an entire team of experts for these Summits. We focus on our 40/20/40 System (Get Out and Create Your Own Legend, the Universe Model of Social Media Marketing, and The Shift from Professional to Infopreneur on Steroids) and do a total business makeover. This is not a how-to course: this is a week-long, total-immersion program where you come away with your business transformed. And you continue to work with a team of expert consultants who assist you as much or as little as you need after the event.

But far more important than any of that, those who attend a PersonalSuccess Summit come away with a very special peer group. There is a real emphasis over this week-long event on building the group into a true InnerCore Mastermind as envisioned by Napoleon Hill in his classic work **Think and Grow Rich**. That peer group is worth more than their collective weight in gold.

When you surround yourself with people who are in the top one percent, they will push you to be more than you ever thought you could be. This is the group that teaches you that real wealth has much more to do with time than money. Your money's real value is in its ability to free your time to pursue your real passion, whatever that is for YOU!

So... what did *you* learn from Maximillion, Max, and all the ideas you found in this book? Are you ready to have Dr. Marc and Charlie take you to *your* Summit? Your time for success is now!

Let Us Know What You Thought About This Book

To Contact Dr. Marc and Charlie To Speak At Your Group: PersonalSuccessMarketing.com

5361650R0

Made in the USA
Charleston, SC
04 June 2010